Successful Common Criteria Evaluations

A Practical Guide for Vendors

Successful Common Criteria Evaluations

A Practical Guide for Vendors

Wesley Hisao Higaki

Successful Common Criteria Evaluations: A Practical Guide for Vendors

Copyright © 2010 by Wesley Hisao Higaki

Cover Design by Yukie Higaki

ISBN

1-4528-8661-X
978-1-4528-8661-9

Printed by CreateSpace

www.createspace.com/3456131

www.successfulCCevaluations.com

Acknowledgments

I would like to thank Ray Potter, Jeremy Epstein and Linda McCarthy for their valuable feedback on the contents and format of this book. I want to especially thank my son, Kazuo, for reviewing the draft and providing a technical outsider's point of view.

I would also like to thank the members of the Common Criteria Vendors' Forum for all of their support and perseverance through the years to improve relations with the Common Criteria Development Board and the U.S. National Information Assurance Partnership. I would like to especially thank Mary Ann Davidson and Steve Lipner for their encouragement over the many years we've worked together.

I give my warmest thanks to my friends and family, especially to my wife, Naomi, for supporting me in everything I do.

About the Cover

Special thanks to my daughter, Yukie, for designing the cover of this book. When we brainstormed ideas about the cover, I explained that to the uninitiated, the Common Criteria evaluation process is sometimes like a maze or labyrinth. She recalled the ancient Greek legend of Theseus and the Minotaur of Crete in the great labyrinth. According to the story, many warriors entered the labyrinth to slay the Minotaur but failed. Theseus not only killed the Minotaur but managed his escape from the labyrinth using a ball of twine. The hedge maze on the book cover represents the complex, labyrinth-like Common Criteria evaluation process and this book is like Theseus' ball of twine that guides the reader to success.

About the Author

Wes Higaki is the chair and co-founder of the Common Criteria Vendors' Forum (CCVF). The CCVF is an informal group of individuals that work for commercial product companies. They gather to discuss issues and to serve as the "voice of industry" to the Common Criteria development process.

As the former director of the Software Assurance and Product Certifications of Symantec Corporation, Wes led a team to ensure the secure development of software products. This included managing the company's internal secure software development and test training, threat modeling, penetration testing and vulnerability management. He led all of the company's Common Criteria, FIPS-140 certifications and ICSA Labs testing efforts.

He served as a spokesman addressing software assurance issues and has been an invited speaker at several conferences. He led several industry working groups dealing with product security certifications.

Wes has over 30 years of technical and managerial experience in the software industry. Prior to Symantec, Wes worked for Axent Technologies and over 20 years in R&D at Hewlett-Packard Company.

Wes received a Bachelor of Science degree in mathematics from the University of California, Davis and a Master of Science degree in computer science from Santa Clara University.

Connect with Wes through LinkedIn.com at:
www.linkedin.com/in/weshigaki

Table of Contents

Table of Figures

Table of Tables

PART 1: BACKGROUND

In this part:

Chapter 1: Introduction

The product manager (PM) for Symantec's Network Access Control (SNAC) called me unexpectedly late one afternoon in the fall of 2007. He explained that a U.S. Army contract was up for renewal and the purchasing agent told him that regulations required that SNAC get a "Common Criteria evaluation" as a prerequisite for renewal. The Army had originally purchased SNAC a couple years earlier when it was a product of Sygate Technologies and at the time they did not require the Common Criteria (CC) evaluation. By 2007, the U.S. Department of Defense (DOD) began enforcing the CC requirement and Symantec acquired Sygate. The PM knew that there were several other hungry competitors waiting for the opportunity to snatch business away from us, so it was important to respond positively to this requirement. The PM asked me, "What is a Common Criteria evaluation?"

For the PM and the Army purchasing agent, the CC is a procurement requirement – a "checkbox." Without it, the PM could not sell additional SNAC licenses to the Army; this would reduce the amount of revenue for the product line. The PM did not care that CC is an international standard for assessing the security of products and a way for customers to gain confidence in the product's ability to withstand cyber attacks; he only cared about protecting his revenue stream. He wanted to know, "How can we get this done?"

My job was to lead the SNAC product development team toward a successful CC product evaluation. Success was determined by a timely and cost-effective completion of the evaluation project culminating in the award of a CC certificate. The key to success was to educate the product development team on the requirements, the process, and their roles and responsibilities then to lead them (and our partners) through the process.

I have gone through this drill many times before with many other product teams. I have been involved with CC product security evaluations since 2001 with Symantec's first CC evaluation - the Symantec Enterprise Firewall 7.0 product. At the time, we didn't know what we were doing and followed the lead of the consultants we hired. It took an extremely long time and cost several hundreds of thousands of dollars. It was never clear to me if we actually recouped our investments through incremental sales or prevented lost sales for all of the effort. Nonetheless, I led 15 successful CC evaluations between 2001 and 2008 and learned a great deal about the CC standards, evaluation process and procurement requirements. I also learned how to efficiently and effectively navigate through the CC process to reduce evaluation costs by 20% through proper preparation and following proven best practices.

Motivation for this Book

I have found that CC evaluations are time-consuming, expensive and have a questionable return-on-investment. I learned that many other commercial product vendors were facing these same issues, so in 2004, Jeremy Epstein and I, along with several representatives from other companies, formed the Common Criteria Vendors' Forum (CCVF) - an informal organization of commercial product vendors from around the world struggling through the CC evaluation process [CCVF]. We continue to meet today to discuss common issues with the CC standards, government regulations and how to collaborate on projects to improve the CC and its implementation around the world. CCVF members live with the shortcomings of the CC, but recognize the importance of retaining an internationally accepted standard for assessing product security. We believe that with all of its faults, CC is worth improving. I continue to chair the CCVF and we have established regular meetings with the U.S. CC Scheme (NIAP) as well as the CC Development Board (CCDB) to develop solutions together.

I am writing this book in the spirit of the CCVF – to share my experiences with this obscure and complex process so that other vendors can navigate through it more easily.

The primary audience for this book is product vendors who are faced with having to undergo their first CC evaluation. By sharing my experiences, I hope to help the reader avoid the pitfalls that might lead to an expensive, unsuccessful evaluation. More experienced vendors also may benefit from the lessons learned through my many experiences across a wide variety of products, governments, evaluation labs and consultants.

How this Book Is Organized

Part 1 of this book gives the reader some essential background information about the CC standards and the overall evaluation process. Part 2 provides insights into how to prepare for a CC evaluation. Part 3 gives guidance on how to prepare evidence documentation for the evaluation. Part 4 shares stories from vendors in real-world experiences.

Part 5 concludes the book with a discussion of the issues facing CC and its possible future.

I will address the key questions many vendors have about CC. I will give information about what the novice should consider when going through this arduous process. I will share my perspectives based on the objectives we set and I hope that this will give the reader some valuable food for thought and some good guidance.

Today, the United States government procurement policies requiring CC evaluation, especially within the U.S. Department of Defense, have attracted much of the attention around CC. Because of that, much of this book is aimed at the issues faced by vendors evaluating their products in the United States for U.S. government customers. Government procurement policies that reference CC evaluations are at the heart of many of the issues vendors face today.

Most of my experience has been with software products built mostly in the United States. While doing my research for this book, I have recognized that the assumptions I've made about "standard" product development practices may not be broadly applicable – especially outside the U.S. I also recognize that other vendors use the CC differently. I will present some of these views as well.

I will conclude this book with a discussion about the issues with the fundamental framework and implementation of CC and what the future perhaps holds for all of us. The Common Criteria has great unrealized potential to be a valuable tool for customers and product vendors but needs to evolve to reach that potential.

Chapter 2: The Common Criteria Standards

Product vendors, engineering managers, product managers and friends frequently ask me, "What is the Common Criteria?" To the Symantec Network Access Control product manager, the Common Criteria (CC) was an Army "checkbox" procurement requirement, but to security experts around the world the CC is an international standard - one that is recognized by 26 different countries. I have always maintained that international recognition is the greatest benefit CC provides. The fact that vendors can have their product CC evaluated once in one country and have that evaluation recognized and accepted in any one of the 26 supporting countries is a huge benefit. During the 1980s when countries such as the U.S. and U.K. had their different security evaluation programs, vendors would have to choose which evaluations they would pursue and thus which countries' governments they could sell to. The cost of each individual evaluation was high, so pursuing multiple evaluations was not practical. The governments recognized this dilemma and unified their evaluation standards under the CC. This unification enabled government customers greater access to state-of-the-art, evaluated products.

The CC standards contain a standard set of security criteria or a security vocabulary so that customers, vendors and evaluators can all use the same terms. Along with the standard vocabulary it has a common language to describe product security characteristics. Moreover, to ensure consistent evaluation and assessment of the products, CC has a standard evaluation methodology. Before we delve into the history and details of the standards, let's discuss why standards and evaluation are important.

The Role of Security Standards and Evaluation

Why does the Common Criteria exist and what purpose does it serve? Mary Ann Davidson, Chief Product Security Officer, at Oracle answers that question with an enlightening statement in an October 7, 2007 *Government Computer News* (GCN) article [Davidson]. Davidson states that IT vendors make proclamations about the security of their products. Without some proof, customers would have to take the vendor's word that their claims are true. The Common Criteria provides value to customers by having independent third-parties validate those vendor claims against internationally-accepted standards.

Customers want confidence that the products they purchase and use will meet their security requirements. Product vendors may assert that they include security features in their products and employ secure development practices. The level of confidence (or assurance) customers gain from vendor assertions depends on how trustworthy the vendors are. Independent confirmation of those vendor claims by third-party evaluators can give customers even greater confidence. Customers can gain even more confidence if those independent, third party evaluations are performed using open standards. Benefits of these types of evaluations include:

- Examination against recognized industry standard metrics and criteria so customers have some confidence that the measures are complete and relevant
- Standardized examination methods so that customers are guaranteed consistent, unbiased results
- Credibility of the third party is the basis for trusting the results. Third parties that use open processes for standards development and publication of results gain the broadest credibility.

Security testing and evaluation standards provide a way to do uniform comparisons of products. Having these standards reduces confusion for the customer so that they are not faced with trying to compare products evaluated under different regimes and criteria. Standards and standard testing also help lower costs to customers; rather than having each customer or even each market segment use their own unique evaluation - an internationally-recognized evaluation will relieve customers of the burden of developing, maintaining and executing evaluations on their own.

A (Very) Brief History of the Common Criteria

Ray Potter, my friend and former counterpart at Cisco Systems, and I used to complain that far too many International Common Criteria Conference (ICCC) presentations began with a "History of the Common Criteria." The excessive rehashing of the history drove us nuts! However, for someone new to CC and for the reader of this book, it is important to know a little bit about the history of how we got to where we are today in order to develop a common language and knowledge and to avoid repeating past mistakes.

I was a software engineering manager for Hewlett-Packard Company (HP) in the mid-1980s and I recall hearing stories of versions of our HP-UX operating system products having to undergo C2 *certification*. At the time, U.S. Department of Defense (DOD) procurement policies required certain products to undergo trusted computer system evaluations. C2 was one of the levels described in the DOD 5200.28 standard (also known as the *Orange Book*). This evaluation process literally took years and HP invested a lot of money towards completing this certification. All of this effort went toward satisfying just one (albeit large) customer's requirement to prove the adequacy of the security of the operating system for their environment. The really big problem was – the DOD wasn't the only one requiring these kinds of costly certifications.

The governments of the United Kingdom (U.K.), Canada, Germany and France also wanted assurance that the products they purchased from commercial vendors would meet their security requirements, so they established similar standards and certification processes as the United States. From a vendor's point of view, this was a huge problem because if it took years and hundreds of thousands of dollars to complete just one evaluation for one customer then it would take that many more times that investment to meet the needs of the other customers. Given the ever-present time-to-market pressures and resource constraints, vendors were forced to choose which customer's certification requirements they could afford to meet. Did they want to meet the requirements of the U.S. or the U.K.? Could they choose between selling to France or Germany? These were some tough decisions to make.

Meanwhile, some of the government agencies were limited to purchasing and using only certified products. As you might imagine, if the state-of-the-art secure products are tied up in the evaluation process for years, the customers would naturally try to find a way to use the products even if they had not completed the evaluation process. The use of waivers became popular (especially in the U.S.) to enable non-certified products to be deployed in government installations. These waivers were a slap in the face to those vendors (such as HP) who devoted sincere effort and expended precious resources to meet the government requirements only to have other vendors slip into government sites ahead of them. More and more vendors lost faith in the DOD program and this spelled the end of the *Orange Book* program.

Successful Common Criteria Evaluations

In the mid-1990s, several nations realized similar situations as the U.S and collaborated to combine their individual national security standards into the Common Criteria for Information Technology Security Evaluation or the *Common Criteria* (CC). This standard was submitted to the International Standards Organization (ISO) and the CC was officially established as ISO 15408 in 1999 and was developed out of these previous approaches:

- Trusted Computing System Evaluation Criteria (TCSEC) - United States DOD 5200.28 Standard also known as the *Orange Book*
- Federal Criteria (FC) – a draft approach developed by the U.S. National Institute of Standards and Technology (NIST) and the National Security Agency (NSA) to replace TCSEC in 1992
- Information Technology Security Evaluation Criteria (ITSEC) - developed in the early 1990s by France, Germany, the Netherlands and the U.K.
- Canadian Trusted Computer Product Evaluation Criteria (CTCPEC) - the Canadian standard first developed in 1993 from the U.S. DOD standard

Today, there are 26 countries participating in the CC program. Each year, the number of participating countries increases as developing nations realize that they can save a lot of redundant effort by following an international standard rather than creating their own evaluation programs.

Participating countries sign the *Common Criteria Mutual Recognition Agreement* (CCRA) which basically states the conditions for participation including the requirement that each member country recognize certificates issued from the other member countries. From the vendor's perspective, this condition is critical and is perhaps the greatest benefit of the CC. Vendors only have to certify their products once and each of the other CCRA member countries will recognize that certificate. This corrects the situation vendors faced in the 1980s where they had to choose which country's evaluation program to pursue.

Each CCRA member nation has a CC governing body or *Scheme* responsible for managing the implementation and use of the CC in their country.

The National Information Assurance Partnership Common Criteria Evaluation and Validation Scheme for IT Security (NIAP CCEVS or NIAP) is the United States' CC Scheme [NIAP]. Many U.S. customers will refer to CC evaluations as *NIAP certifications*.

Chapter 2: The Common Criteria Standards

NIAP was originally formed as a collaborative effort between the U.S. National Institute of Technology and Standards (NIST) and the U.S. National Security Agency (NSA) with the following objectives:

- To meet the needs of government and industry for cost-effective evaluation of IT products
- To encourage the formation of commercial security testing laboratories and the development of a private sector security testing industry
- To ensure that security evaluations of IT products are performed to consistent standards
- To improve the availability of evaluated IT products

Initially, NIST's role was to represent civilian agencies' security requirements while the NSA provided the DOD and intelligence agencies requirements. NIST also leveraged their National Voluntary Laboratory Accreditation Program (NVLAP) to accredit the CC evaluation testing labs (CCTL). NVLAP accreditations require the CC evaluation labs to demonstrate adherence to certain standards. For a variety of reasons, NIST's involvement in NIAP has all but vanished. Today, NIAP is funded entirely by the NSA and sponsoring DOD agencies. Organizationally, NIAP is now under the commercial systems department of the information assurance directorate.

There are two types of CCRA member nations. There are *certificate-authorizing* countries which have been approved to issue the CC certificates. The other nations are known as *certificate-consuming* countries which do not issue certificates but recognize them. As a vendor, you can take your product for CC evaluation to evaluation labs at any of the *certificate-authorizing* countries and the certification will be recognized by any of the 26 nations in the CCRA. The CCRA *certificate-consuming* nations and their governing Schemes are shown in Table 1. Table 2 lists *certificate-authorizing* nations.

Certificate Consuming	Scheme
Austria	Federal Chancellery operated by Federal Ministry of Public Service and Sports
The Czech Republic	National Security Authority of the Czech Republic
Denmark	National IT and Telecom Agency
Finland	Ministry of Finance
Greece	Ministry of Interior
Hungary	Ministry of IT and Telecommunication
India	Government of India Department of Information Technology
Israel	Standards Institution of Israel
Malaysia	CyberSecurity Malaysia (formerly known as NISER)
Pakistan	Ministry of Defence
Singapore	Infocomm Development Authority of Singapore (IDA)
Turkey	TSE (Turkish Standards Institution)

Table 1: Certificate Consuming Nations

Certificate Authorizing	Scheme
Australia	Australasian Information Security Evaluation Program (AISEP) operated by the Defence Signals Directorate
New Zealand	
Canada	Canadian Common Criteria Evaluation and Certification Scheme operated by the Communications Security Establishment (CSE)
France	Agence Nationale de la Sécurité des Systèmes d'Information (ANSSI)
Germany	German Evaluation and Certification Scheme operated by Bundesamt für Sicherheit in der Informationstechnik (BSI)
Italy	Autorità Nazionale per la Sicurezza
Japan	Japanese Evaluation and Certification Scheme operated by the Japan Information Technology Security Evaluation and Certification Scheme (JISEC)
Republic of Korea (South Korea)	Korea IT Security Evaluation and Certification Scheme (KECS) operated by the National Intelligence Service (NIS)
The Netherlands	Netherlands National Communications Security Agency (NLNCSA)
Norway	Norwegian Certification Authority for IT Security (SERTIT) operated by the Norwegian National Security Authority
Spain	Organismo de Certificación de la Seguridad de las Tecnologías de la Información
Sweden	The Swedish Common Criteria Evaluation and Certification Scheme operated by the Swedish Certification Body for IT Security (CSEC)
United Kingdom	U.K. IT Security Evaluation and Certification Scheme operated by The Communications-Electronics Security Group (CESG)
United States of America	Common Criteria Evaluation and Validation Scheme (CCEVS) under the National Information Assurance Partnership (NIAP)

Table 2: Certificate Authorizing Nations

In the 1980s, evaluations were performed exclusively by government agencies that could not handle the volume of work placed before them. This exacerbated the delays vendors and customers endured. To address this issue, national CC Schemes now accredit independent, commercial CC evaluation laboratories to conduct the actual product evaluations. Product vendors contract with these labs to perform CC evaluations and the national Scheme issues the certificates upon successful completion.

The graph in Figure 1 shows the growth (and decline over recent years) of the number of CC evaluations world-wide. The spike in 2006-2007 may be attributed to the U.S. government reinforcement of their stated policies requiring CC evaluations as a condition for procurement. The more recent declines may be a result of the overall decline in the global economy or perhaps some dwindling interest in CC evaluated products. The data used to generate this graph came from the CC Portal [CC Portal] in April 2010.

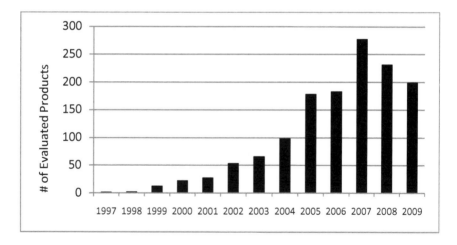

Figure 1: CC Evaluated Products By Year

The Common Criteria Development Board (CCDB) is responsible for improving, enhancing and revising the CC standards. The CCDB is composed of representatives from the various national CC Schemes. The CCDB revises the CC standards documents, publishes them for review, and finalizes them. This process is independent of the International Standards Organization (ISO) process except that the CCDB submits final CC standards to ISO to be accepted as ISO standards. The

ISO standards are important because the European and Asian nations in particular use the ISO standards as the basis for their work. The U.S. tends to use the latest CC standards.

The current ISO standard ISO/IEC 14508-2009 is based on CC version 3.1. For all practical purposes, the CC standards are the ones to watch. The CC standards documents are downloadable from the Common Criteria Portal website free of charge; however, ISO typically charges for their standards documents.

The Common Criteria Framework

The Common Criteria provides an internationally-recognized framework to describe and evaluate security attributes of a product. The Common Criteria language provides a vocabulary and format for expressing customer security requirements and vendor product claims. The *Common Evaluation Methodology* (CEM) provides direction for evaluators to perform consistent security evaluations. The CC standards [CC Standards] documents capture these descriptions in 4 parts.

- CC Part 1 – Introduction and General Model
- CC Part 2 – Security Functional Components
- CC Part 3 – Security Assurance Components
- Common Evaluation Methodology (CEM)

While reading the CC standards is a bit like reading a dictionary or a rather dry textbook, it is important to have some level of under-standing for what is contained in them. The following section provides an overview of each of the 4 parts of the CC standards highlighting the importance and relevance of each from the vendor's perspective (as opposed to a security purist's or academic's point of view.)

> **Evaluation, Certification and Validation**
>
> I will frequently use the term *evaluation* and occasionally use the term *certification* or *validation* in this book. Evaluation is the set of activities the evaluation lab performs to assess your product against security claims you make. This is the complex and sometimes arcane process that has caused many vendors heartache over the years.
>
> Once the evaluation lab is satisfied that your product meets the claims you make, the evaluation process is complete. The evaluation results are sent to the national government CC Scheme to be certified. The U.S. government prefers to use the term *validated* for products because *certified* refers to systems. However, the rest of the world uses the term *certified* here. In this book, consider both of these terms to be synonymous.

CC Part 1: Introduction and General Model

CC Part 1 [CC Standards] lays out the framework for how the CC works. This document explains the objectives of the CC, the basic philosophy of the evaluation process (model), and definitions of the key components of the CC. The introduction of Part 1 explains that the CC provides a standard set of IT security characteristics for functionality and assurance. These security characteristics are used during security evaluations whereby the results enable comparisons of the independent evaluations.

The CC evaluations provide a specified level of confidence that the claimed security functionality will meet customer needs. Armed with this information, customers can make more informed purchasing decisions.

The CC framework was designed to be relevant to a wide variety of IT products – computers, networking products, operating systems, databases and application software. This characteristic probably was also created out of the need to satisfy the needs of several nations (i.e. U.S., U.K., Canada, France, Germany and the Netherlands – the founders of the CC). In principle, customers can select any combination of attributes from the CC standards to express their security needs; product vendors can use those same attributes to make their security claims. There is even a provision to include *explicitly-stated* or custom attributes in case none of the standard set of components applies.

CC Is Not Perfect

The CC is based on many years of research and past implementations by the various governments and represents a significant investment in time and resources. In spite of my criticisms of the CC, it would be foolhardy for anyone else to attempt to replicate this effort. I will discuss some of the issues and challenges still facing the CC in Chapter 19: Issues with the Common Criteria, but for all of its faults, I think it is better than anything else we have to assess the security of products.

CC Part 1 includes an extensive dictionary of CC terms – 15 pages worth. This is the place to go for the explanations for any term, acronym or abbreviation used in the standards.

The general model descriptions in CC Part 1 illustrate some of the underlying philosophy behind the CC evaluation process. CC is based on providing customers assurance by evaluating products and evidence rather than through theoretical modeling and simulation. Moreover, CC uses "after-the-fact" evaluation - that is, evaluating the product after it has been developed or evaluating evidence (e.g. design documents) after that product development phase has been completed. This is in contrast to evaluating the development process while it is ongoing. I liken the CC evaluation process to financial auditing – outsiders examining your financial records and documented procedures to determine if you did what you said you did.

In order to understand the CC language, it is important to realize that IT organizations have assets they want to protect; those assets are subject to threats; those threats can be mitigated by countermeasures. The CC language gives us the tools necessary to articulate the threats and countermeasures.

Protection Profiles

A *Protection Profile* (PP) is a document describing the security requirements for a given product type such as operating systems and firewalls. Protection Profiles are generally developed by groups of users, vendors and/or governments.

The bulk of certified PPs are from the U.S. government and the Smart Card Industry. The following are some of the approved PPs:

- Anti-Virus
- Certificate Management
- Databases
- Disk Encryption
- Intrusion Detection System/Intrusion Prevention System
- Firewall
- Operating System
- Peripheral Switch
- Router
- USB Encryption
- Virtual Private Network
- Wireless LAN
- Enterprise Security Management
- Enterprise Firewall
- Security IC Platform (Smart Card)

Vendors can evaluate their products against the requirements in one of these applicable PPs or they can make their own claims and have those claims assessed through the CC evaluation process. NIAP and other international government agencies have established policies requiring some products to only evaluate against applicable PPs.

Security Target and Target of Evaluation

A *Security Target* (ST) is the document produced by the vendor describing the security claims about their product. These claims may be in response to a PP or these claims may merely be vendor assertions. In either case, the product can be evaluated and certified. If you think of a PP as the security marketing requirements document (MRD), then the ST is the security engineering requirements document (ERD) or how the product addresses the customer requirements.

A key term used in the ST is the *Target of Evaluation* (TOE). The TOE is the focus of the evaluation. All of the security claims that will be evaluated must be met by the TOE. That is, the TOE is the subset of the product that contains all of the security-relevant functionality.

The ST document is the foundation of the CC evaluation; it frames the scope of the evaluation and describes the vendor security claims. All of the evaluation effort is based on information provided in the ST. The ST document is organized as follows:

Chapter 2: The Common Criteria Standards

- Introduction
- Conformance claims
- Security problem definition
- Security objectives
- Extended components definition
- Security requirements
- TOE Summary Specification

CC Part 2: Security Functional Components

As a language, the CC standards have a standard vocabulary. The standard vocabulary enables customers to express their security needs and vendors to articulate the security characteristics of their product in a consistent manner. The first set of security characteristics defined by CC [CC Standards], the *Security Functional Requirements* (SFR), are standard identifiers and descriptions of security features about the product itself. These security features are the counter-measures to *threats*. For example, there is an SFR for defining how the product will protect user data by using access controls. SFRs are organized into 11 major groups called *Security Functional Classes*. Ostensibly, these classes define all of the potential security functions a product could provide. The *Security Functional Classes* from CC Part 2 are listed in Table 3.

Class ID	Class Name	Description
FAU	Security Audit	Security event audit record handling
FCO	Communications	Non-repudiation of origin and receipt
FCS	Cryptographic Support	Cryptographic operation and key management
FDP	User Data Protection	Protecting user data transferred within the TOE
FIA	Identification and Authentication	User identification and authentication
FMT	Security Management	Management of TOE security functions, attributes and data
FPR	Privacy	Includes anonymity, pseudonymity, unlinkability and unobservability
FPT	Protection of the TSF	Protect TSF data. Recovery and self-test

FRU	Resource Utilization	Includes fault tolerance, service priority and resource allocation
FTA	TOE Access	Restricts access to TOE
FTP	Trusted Paths/Channels	Trusted communications paths and channels with the TSF

Table 3: Functional Classes

The *Classes* are further segmented into several *families, components* and *elements*. The SFRs contained within CC Part 2 represent decades of effort to identify, describe and categorize effective counter-measures to a wide variety of IT threats. A great deal of effort has gone into developing this "dictionary" of security functions. Using these standard requirements helps remove the ambiguity of using different terms for the same requirement. To accommodate a wide variety of product types and security features, SFRs may include *operations* that further refine the definitions.

Some SFRs have dependencies. That is, using an SFR which has dependencies means you must also include those dependencies. For example, *Authentication Failure Handling* (FIA_AFL.1.1) has a dependency on *Timing of Authentication* (FIA_UID.1.1). This means that if you claim that your product supports FIA_AFL.1.1 you must also claim that your product supports FIA_UID.1.1 as well. The dependency makes sense because if you are going to try to lock someone out after a specified number of failed login attempts (as FIA_AFL.1.1 states), you must first allow the authenticated login before the user is identified (as required by FIA_UID.1.1).

Terminology

A somewhat annoying thing I found in reading the CC standards is the use of terms such as *can, informative, may, normative, shall* and *should*; these terms have precise meanings as defined in ISO/IEC Directives, Part 2 [ISO]. You should be aware of the nuances of each of these terms as they appear in the CC standards. The precise definition of these terms as they are used in the SFRs will dictate whether your product actually meets certain requirements or not.

CC Part 3: Security Assurance Components

The reason CC exists is to improve customer confidence (assurance) in the security of the IT products they purchase and use. That confidence is obtained by not only providing security features (SFRs) in the product but also providing security in the product development processes. CC Part 3 [CC Standards] states that CC gains assurance through the evaluation of development processes.

The foundation of CC is to provide assurance through the use of independent evaluation techniques. When applied to evaluating development processes, these evaluation techniques include:

- Examination and analysis of the soundness of vendor development procedures and processes
- Check for the application and adherence to those processes
- Analysis and comparison of the various TOE design evidence
- Comparison of the evidence against the security requirements
- Validation of claims
- Analysis of user guidance
- Analysis of product tests
- Perform independent functional tests
- Vulnerability analysis
- Penetration testing

Where CC Part 2 and the SFRs are used to describe security characteristics about the product itself, CC Part 3 and the security assurance components relate to the security of the product development processes. The *Security Assurance Requirements* (SAR) cover areas regarding the secure development, delivery and deployment of the product. The eight *Security Assurance Classes* described in CC Part 3 are listed in Table 4.

Class ID	Class Name	Description
ADV	Development	Product architecture, functional specifications, internals, implementation and design
AGD	Guidance Documents	Operation and installation guides
ALC	Lifecycle Support	Configuration management, delivery, development, flaw remediation security
ATE	Tests	Test coverage, depth. Functional and independent testing
AVA	Vulnerability Assessment	Vulnerability analysis
ACO	Composition	Composition evidence, testing, vulnerability analysis and rationale

Table 4: Assurance Classses

Security Assurance Classes are segmented into *families, components* and *elements*. For example, the ADV, *Development* class is broken down into the following *families*:

- Security Architecture (ADV_ARC)
- Functional Specification (ADV_FSP)
- Implementation Representation (ADV_IMP)
- TOE Security Function Internals (ADV_INT)
- Security Policy Modeling (ADV_SPM)
- TOE Security Design (ADV_TDS)

Each of the *families* is further decomposed into *components* and *elements* that provide the details of the specific requirements.

The SAR notation also has *D, C* and *E element identifiers*. These denote requirements for **D**evelopers, **C**ontent and **E**valuators respectively. Developers are the product developers or vendors. Content is the evidence documentation produced for evaluation. Evaluators are the independent third-party evaluators.

For example, ADV_INT.3.1, *Minimally Complex internals*, requires the developer to design and implement the *Target of Evaluation Security Functionality* (TSF) using well-structured internals. A TSF can be something like a user authentication mechanism to detect or prevent unauthorized access to the system. Developers who use structured design methodologies will be able to claim that they support this requirement. The content and presentation elements are the evidence (documentation) presented to the evaluators to prove that the requirement has been met. Finally, the evaluators shall confirm the claims made by the developers. The CEM document goes into much more detail on the evaluator's actions and requirements.

You might think that as a vendor you don't need to worry about what the evaluator requirements are in these SARs. However, you may save yourself some time and cost if you read the evaluator requirements in not only Part 3 but in the CEM as well to find out precisely what the evaluator is going to be looking for to satisfy each requirement.

Assurance Level	Description
EAL 1	Functionally Tested
EAL 2	Structurally Tested
EAL 3	Methodically Tested and Checked
EAL 4	Methodically Designed, Tested and Reviewed
EAL 5	Semi-Formally Designed and Tested
EAL 6	Semi-Formally Verified Design and Tested
EAL 7	Formally Verified Design and Tested

Table 5: EAL Descriptions

Evaluation Assurance Levels (EAL) were created as a convenient collection of SARs denoting seven different levels of evaluation assurance. Generally speaking, EALs are used rather than individual SARs to define assurance requirements. Table 5 illustrates the seven levels range from least stringent (EAL 1) to most stringent (EAL 7). The idea here is that a customer can look at the EAL of an evaluated product and tell at a glance how much effort went into the assessment of the security claims made by the vendor. Most commercial products will evaluate their products at EAL 2 to EAL 4. EAL 4 is the highest level that is mutually recognized internationally. The belief is that evaluations higher than EAL 4 require unique or proprietary evaluation techniques that cannot be duplicated or standardized internationally.

EALs may also be *augmented* by adding SARs to the assurance claims. For example, adding the SAR ALC_FLR.1, Basic Flaw Remediation, to EAL 2 would be denoted *EAL 2 augmented with ALC_FLR.1* or more informally *EAL 2+*. This means that in addition to the SARs contained within the standard EAL 2 requirements, ALC_FLR.1 is added as illustrated in Table 6.

Security Assurance Class	Assurance Components	Description
Development	ADV_ARC.1	Security architecture description
	ADV_FSP.2	Security-enforcing functional specification
	ADV_TDS.1	Basic design
Guidance Documents	AGD_OPE.1	Operational user guidance
	AGD_PRE.1	Preparative guidance
Life-Cycle Support	ALC_CMC.2	Use of a CM system
	ALC_CMS.2	Parts of the TOE CM coverage
	ALC_DEL.1	Delivery procedures
	ALC_FLR.1	Basic flaw remediation
Tests	ATE_COV.1	Evidence of coverage
	ATE_FUN.1	Functional testing
	ATE_IND.2	Independent testing - simple
Vulnerability Assessment	AVA_VAN.2	Vulnerability analysis

Table 6: EAL 2 Augmented with ALC_FLR.1 Requirements

The notion of different assurance levels comes from the CC foundational belief that assurance (i.e. customer confidence) is driven by evaluation and that more in-depth evaluation will give customers greater confidence. In theory, the higher the EAL used during the evaluation, the greater confidence the customer should have that the claims made by the vendor are true. Evaluations at higher EALs require more detailed evidence and greater evaluator scrutiny; these activities should provide greater proof of the vendor claims.

Competing companies and customers have mistakenly used the EAL to be equivalent to the security "grade" of the product. Some believe that an EAL 4 evaluated product is more secure than an EAL 3 evaluated product. This is not necessarily true. EAL 4 means there will be more evidence produced and more evaluation effort exerted than EAL 3, but it says nothing about the security functions (SFR) within each product. Many seasoned veterans of the CC sarcastically say that the EAL number is a just measure of the depth of the stack of documentation you had to write for the evaluation. Documentation does not make the product more secure. There does seem to be a need for our customers to more easily grade the security of our products, but EALs are not the way to accomplish this.

Common Evaluation Methodology (CEM)

The *Common Evaluation Methodology* (CEM) [CC Standards] is the standardized instructions to the evaluation labs on how to evaluate the different assurance requirements. The CEM tells the evaluator what to look for and to what depth s/he should evaluate the evidence. Depending on the EAL, the evaluator will examine evidence to varying depths. Evaluators are instructed to *check, examine, record* and *report*; each term has a specific meaning as defined by the CEM as:

- *check* - generate a verdict by a simple comparison
- *examine* - generate a verdict by analysis using evaluator expertise
- *record* - retain a written description of procedures, events, observations, insights and results in sufficient detail to enable the work performed during the evaluation to be reconstructed at a later time
- *report* - include evaluation results and supporting material in the Evaluation Technical Report or an Observation Report

As you can see, even the definitions may be subject to interpretation and variance based on the evaluator's experience. Some of the potential variance is mitigated because many of the evaluators have a common background (e.g. military or government security experience) or because of a common understanding that is not captured in any documentation.

Even though the CC Part 3 document describes evaluator actions for each SAR, the CEM provides much more detailed instructions on what they have to do to satisfy the evaluation requirement. This level of detail helps ensure greater consistency across evaluators and across international Schemes.

Summary

Here are some of the key concepts and terms to remember from the CC standards:

Target of Evaluation (TOE) is the focus of the evaluation. It is usually a subset of a product's security functionality.

Security Functional Requirements (SFR) are the product security functions that will be evaluated. Examples are: user identification and authentication mechanisms, data protection, security configuration and audit logging features.

Security Assurance Requirements (SAR) define the characteristics of product secure development, delivery, deployment and maintenance processes.

Evaluation Assurance Levels (EAL) are collections of SARs that define varying levels of evaluation scrutiny. SARs are defined with increasing levels of evaluation depth requiring more evidence and more evaluation effort.

Security Target (ST) is the first document the developer produces and is evaluated. It includes the security claims (SFR) and describes the TOE that will be evaluated.

Protection Profile (PP) is a document produced to capture customer security requirements (SFR).

Common Evaluation Methodology (CEM) is part 4 of the CC standards documents and describes the actions required of the evaluators.

Chapter 3: Process Overview

Before beginning any journey, it is useful to have a map to guide you. It is important to understand where you are, where you want to go, and how to get to your final destination. CC evaluations are journeys that require preparation and activities to move you forward toward reaching the goal. Every product development team I've worked with wants to know what the steps are to complete a CC evaluation. In this chapter I will give an overview of the phases involved in a CC evaluation plus the on-going assurance maintenance phase. The major phases of the evaluation and validation process are:

Phase 0: Pre-evaluation preparation
Phase 1: Project launch
Phase 2: Evaluation and feedback
Phase 3: Validation and certification
Phase 4: Assurance maintenance

Phase 0: Pre-Evaluation Preparation

Phase 0 of the CC evaluation process is what I call "pre-evaluation preparation" that will be covered in much more detail in Part 2 of this book. Pre-evaluation preparation is one of the key elements to completing CC evaluations efficiently. Like any project or journey, proper preparation ensures a successful result. Pre-evaluation preparation activities include: researching customer requirements, understanding the CC standards, developing a compelling business case, managing the project's scope, allocating resources and selecting partners. These activities will establish a solid foundation upon which to build the CC evaluation project including knowledge, resources, goals and risk minimization.

Phase 1: Project Launch

The Project Launch phase includes all of the activities to prepare for the "kickoff" meeting with the Scheme. The "kickoff" meeting is the formal and official launch of the CC evaluation. It indicates that the evaluation lab and the government validators have approved the project. The key deliverable for this phase and the foundation of the CC evaluation is the *Security Target* (ST). We will discuss the details of the ST later in this book, but here are some considerations for planning purposes.

Security Target

The ST document frames the CC evaluation effort. In essence it answers the question – What is being evaluated? I think of the ST as the foundation upon which all of the rest of the CC evidence documentation is built and that which drives all of the evaluation activities. The standard format of the ST is discussed later in this book but in essence, the ST must describe:

1. Target of Evaluation
2. Evaluated Environment
3. Evaluation Level

Target of Evaluation

The *Target of Evaluation* (TOE) is the product or the subset of the product that is being evaluated. I say "subset of the product" because in most CC evaluation projects I've led the TOE was not the entire product that we delivered to customers. For example, several of our products integrated third-party databases. We shipped this third-party code to our customers as part of our application software but had no way of providing CC evaluation evidence for it. It was impractical for us to make claims about the third-party database, so we excluded it from the TOE.

I have found that a good block diagram (such as the example in Figure 2) depicting the overall product architecture with the TOE bounded by a dotted line (the *TOE boundary*) makes it easier to explain the scope of the evaluation to everyone. This high-level block diagram should include all of the major components whether they are part of the TOE or not. Interfaces between the components should be clearly marked. The ST should then describe (in words) each component. Be sure not to leave anything out; evaluators hate it when you put something in a picture and then don't describe it.

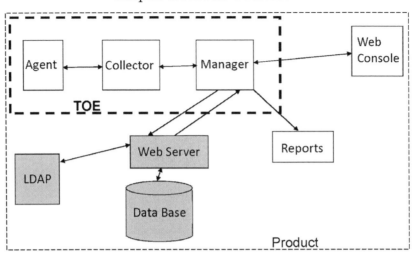

Figure 2: Sample TOE Diagram

The other major aspects about the TOE in the ST are the *Security Functional Requirements* (SFR). These SFRs are the security functions provided by the TOE that will be evaluated. The standard set of SFRs is documented in the CC Part 2.

Security Functional Requirements

Even though CC calls them *Security Functional Requirements*, they are not really requirements; they are claims or attributes - I never figured out why the CC authors chose the word *requirements* here. For product developers *requirements* mean something that has to be in the product; SFRs are just claims we make about the product.

We'll cover *Protection Profiles* (PP) in more detail later but if you decide to evaluate against the requirements in a PP, you will have to use all of the SFRs that are contained in that document. The good news is that all you have to do is copy-and-paste the SFRs directly from the PP.

Explicitly-Stated SFRs

The CC is so flexible that it allows you to not only select which SFRs from CC Part 2 you want but you can also create your own custom or explicitly-stated SFRs. I don't particularly like the use of these types of SFRs because I believe it erodes the CC standards. If you can't find an SFR that is exactly what you are looking for in CC Part 2, then I would think the appropriate action would be to propose a modification to the standard, not make up new stuff! Customers will only be confused by the use of non-standard, explicitly-stated SFRs.

Evaluated Environment

The evaluated environment is the IT and computing environment in which your product is deployed and operated. The ST describes the operational environment – the computer hardware, operating system and network to be used in the evaluation. Evaluated environments attempt to mirror "typical" customer deployments to lend credibility to the evaluation and to leverage "typical" or default configurations that can reduce the effort needed to prepare for the evaluation.

We occasionally included multiple operating system platforms in our CC evaluations because customers specifically asked for them. I had a customer demand that the CC evaluation include Solaris and Windows Server because he planned to deploy the evaluated product on both operating systems. Most of the time however, we chose the "most popular" operating system as our evaluation platform. As I will discuss later in this book, minimizing the scope of the evaluation is a key to success. For the most part, computer hardware selection was not an issue – I guess because our applications were so far removed from the hardware.

CC certificates are only valid for a single product version. Each certificate denotes the specific product version number. Many government procurement officers are particular about making sure that the product version they are ordering is the same as the one that has the CC certificate, so selecting the right product version to evaluate is an important decision.

Strive to maximize the amount of time a product's CC certificate is valid. That is, since new (major) product versions were coming out every year or so and CC evaluations take 9 to 12 months (or longer) it is important to try to time the CC evaluations so as to minimize the time between product release and completing the evaluation.

Evaluation Level

The last major component of the ST is the evaluation assurance level (EAL). Again, if you are evaluating against a Protection Profile, the PP will dictate what EAL against which you must evaluate. Recall (see Chapter 2: The Common Criteria Standards) that the EALs are standard sets of *Security Assurance Requirements* (SAR) that determines the breadth and depth the evaluators will check or examine the evidence. EALs range from level 1 (least stringent) to EAL 7 (most stringent). Generally speaking, the higher the EAL the longer the evaluation will take.

EAL 2 as the Baseline

If you have a choice and you are a novice, I would suggest that you aim your first CC evaluation at EAL 2. In my estimation, if you are in a mature, commercial business your organization should have little trouble meeting the requirements of EAL 2. EAL deals with examining the secure development, delivery and deployment processes. I would say that for most organizations, unless they are very security-conscious that EAL 4 would not be attainable without some changes in the way they develop products.

Evaluation Work Plan

The *Evaluation Work Plan* (EWP) is a plan developed by the CC evaluation lab, developer and CC consultant. It outlines who will deliver what by when. This is an initial plan that will likely change and be adjusted throughout the CC evaluation project. Table 7 shows an example EWP which is basically a preliminary time table of evaluation deliverables.

CC Assurance Class/Family		Target Delivery Date
Security Target (ASE)		13 August 2007
Configuration Management (ACM)	Capability (CAP) – Configuration Identification and CM System Evidence	27 September 2007
Delivery and Operation (ADO)	Delivery (DEL)	27 September 2007
	Installation, Generation and Start-up (IGS)	27 September 2007
Life Cycle Support (ALC)	Flaw Remediation (FLR)	27 September 2007
Guidance Documents (AGD)	Administrator (ADM)	5 October 2007
	User (USR)	5 October 2007
Development (ADV)	Functional Specification (FSP)	9 November 2007
	High-Level Design (HLD)	9 November 2007
	Representation Correspondence (RCR)	9 November 2007
Tests (ATE)	Test Coverage (COV)	9 November 2007
	Developer Tests (FUN)	9 November 2007
Vulnerability Assessment (AVA)	Strength of Function (SOF)	20 February 2008
	Vulnerability Analysis (VLA)	20 February 2008
	Misuse Potential (MSU)	20 February 2008

Table 7: Sample Evaluation Work Plan

Kickoff Meeting with the Scheme

While the kickoff meeting with the Scheme is largely a formality since the preparation for it should have addressed any issues, it is the first major milestone of the CC evaluation. Each Scheme will have its own unique requirements for preparing for and completing the kickoff meeting. The kickoff is the first visible indicator to everyone (including customers and competitors) that this CC evaluation is underway.

Each national Scheme will have their own criteria for accepting products into formal evaluation status, but the U.S. has recently established criteria described in NIAP CCEVS Policy Letter #10 "Acceptance of Security Targets (STs) into NIAP CCEVS Evaluation" dated 22 January 2010.

The purpose of CCEVS Policy Letter #10 was to improve the clarity of the Target of Evaluation (TOE) boundary and expected security attributes prior to acceptance into evaluation. This letter was prompted presumably because of a problem with the quality of Security Targets

(ST) submitted in the past. The apparent lack of clarity in the TOE definition caused problems for evaluations. This policy letter required Common Criteria Testing Labs (CCTL) to verify that any submitted ST contains a clearly defined TOE. Moreover, the ST must:

- Claim compliance with an applicable U.S. Government-approved Protection Profile
- Contain a clear and complete description of the TOE physical and logical boundaries
- Contain a clear definition of components both within and outside of the TOE

NIAP reserves the right to deny acceptance into evaluation if key security functions of a product are left out of the TOE.

Clearly, NIAP is placing restrictions of products entering into evaluation. This is due in part to budgetary constraints at NIAP and abuse by vendors in the past. Some vendors had engaged CC evaluation labs, submitted minimalist STs, and never make progress or completed the evaluations. Meanwhile, NIAP contracted validators who ended up wasting their time. This cost NIAP money – money they could not afford to squander. Vendors did this so that they could claim to their customers that they were *In Evaluation* and gain leverage for sales.

To help prepare for the kickoff meeting, NIAP offers an example agenda for an evaluation acceptance kickoff meeting [Kickoff]. The agenda includes the following items:

- Purpose of the meeting
- Introduction of participants
- Identify roles and responsibilities of the various parties
- Identify key points of contact
- Review the NIAP organization and goals
- Sponsor/vendor introduces the product (TOE)
- Review sponsor/vendor schedules
- Review evaluation plans and schedule
- Review expectations and goals
- Plan future meetings
- Address questions or concerns
- Acceptance into *"In Evaluation"*

Soon after the successful kickoff meeting, many Schemes and some CC evaluation labs will list products on their websites as *In*

Evaluation. This milestone can be an important sales tool since it is publicly visible and represents a strong commitment to customers that you are serious about this CC evaluation. To supplement this, I have issued letters to customers advising them directly that the product has met this milestone. The evaluation lab can now officially begin the evaluation.

Phase 2: Evaluation and Feedback

The Evaluation and Feedback phase is a series of cycles of evidence production, evaluation, comment, modification, resubmission and re-evaluation iterated until the evaluator is satisfied that the requirements for evaluation are complete. The following tasks are performed on each evidence document deliverable.

- Evidence production by the CC consultant with input from the development team
- Evaluation by the CC evaluation lab personnel
- Comments on the evidence by the CC evaluation lab sent back to the vendor
- Modification of the evidence to address the comments
- Resubmission of the evidence
- Re-evaluation by the CC evaluation lab

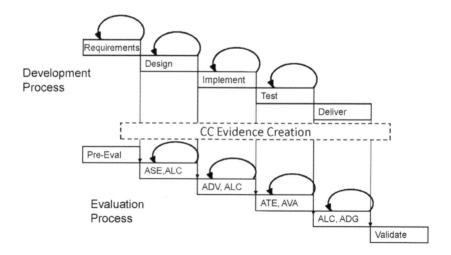

Figure 3: Development and Evaluation Processes

Chapter 3: Process Overview

Figure 3 shows how evaluation evidence may be developed in parallel with the evaluation and synchronized with the product development efforts. This is my preferred method so as to maximize the length of time before the CC evaluated product is replaced by a newer version. The South Korean government however, expects all of the evidence documentation to be delivered to them at the beginning of the evaluation. They seem to have a different model about how CC evaluations and product development cycles work.

The figure also illustrates the evaluation *work units* and their abbreviations including:

- Security Target (ASE)
- Configuration Management (ACM)
- Delivery and Operation (ADO)
- Guidance Documents (AGD)
- Lifecycle Support (ALC)
- Development (ADV)
- Tests (ATE)
- Vulnerability Assessment (AVA)

Each work unit involves the evaluation of one or more evidence documents that are intended to support the vendor claims in the ST. Evidence documentation builds upon each other to provide support of the arguments that the TOE meets the security claims. For example, the ST will claim that the TOE supports a security function such as data protection. The functional specification (part of Development) documentation must describe the data protection functions. Further, the internal design documents must support and be consistent with the functional specifications of the data protection features. The test plans must illustrate how the data protection features were tested.

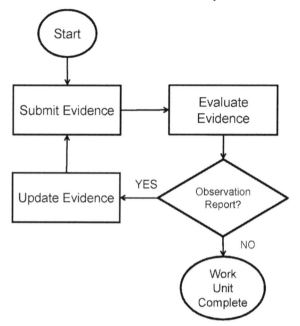

Figure 4: Evidence Evaluation Process

Should the evaluator find an inconsistency or some missing information or an error in the evidence documentation submitted during any work unit, s/he will produce an Observation Report (OR) and send it to the vendor. The OR will typically point out the inconsistency or error, but will not give much information to the vendor on how to rectify the situation. That information would amount to consulting and thus would conflict with the evaluator's objective, third-party role in the evaluation process. I've run into situations where the OR says something as ambiguous as "Functional specifications are inconsistent with ST claims." It was up to me (or our CC consultant) to understand how the functional specifications were inconsistent and what to do about it. The flowchart in Figure 4 shows the iteration through evidence revision cycles until the evaluator is satisfied.

CC evaluation labs are required to produce and send reports to the national Scheme. These reports are called *Evaluation Test Reports* (ETR) and they basically summarize the evaluation progress including the status and disposition of issues and comments reported to the vendor. A final ETR is submitted to the Scheme when all of the evaluation activity work units have been completed.

Site Visit

For most evaluations, the CC evaluator will visit the vendor's development site to observe at least the use of the configuration management system (part of the ALC_CMC work unit). Oftentimes, the evaluators will take this opportunity to check out other things such as testing and delivery procedures. This visit will require dedicated time from the development and QA staff to answer questions from the evaluator and to demonstrate the use of development, build, test and delivery systems. Most site visits take 2 to 5 days depending on the EAL and the complexity of the product or development environment. If your development team is distributed across several sites, the CC evaluator may want to visit those other sites to make sure that the procedures at each site meet the stated (EAL) requirements.

Phase 3: Validation and Certification

When the Scheme receives the final ETR from the CC evaluation lab, the validators will review (i.e. validate) the results, ask questions of the evaluation lab, and decide whether the evaluation successfully met all of the requirements or not. In the U.S., validators (through the Validation Oversight Board) will be monitoring evaluations throughout the process. This monitoring will generally catch any major issues during the process thus avoiding any unwelcome surprises at the end.

When the validators and the Scheme have completed their final review and all issues have been resolved, the CC certificate is issued by the Scheme and awarded to the product vendor. The ST, final certification report, and a copy of the CC certificate are usually posted on the Scheme's website and on the Common Criteria Portal website [CC Portal]. A physical copy of the CC certificate is often presented to the vendor at the annual International Common Criteria Conference or other public events. Copies of certificates can be found on the Common Criteria Portal website.

Waiting For Validation

For the vendor, the validation phase is mostly about just sitting around – waiting. Generally, if the Scheme has any questions, comments or issues, they will take it up with the CC evaluation lab. I've had to wait as little as 2 weeks and as long as 2 months for the validation to be completed.

Phase 4: Assurance Maintenance

As mentioned earlier, CC certificates are only valid for a single version of a product. Many commercial products today are revised every 6 to 18 months. Depending on the complexity of the product and the depth of the evaluation, CC evaluations can take longer than it takes to develop a new revision, thus making the certificate useless. The assurance maintenance mechanism was created to address this situation. While each nation seems to implement this provision slightly differently, the objective is to shorten the re-evaluation cycle for previously evaluated products.

Basically, the vendor must provide evidence that changes in the newer version of the product do not compromise the security claims and evidence presented in the prior version's evaluation. An *Impact Analysis Report* (IAR) is submitted to the same CC evaluation lab that performed the original evaluation. The IAR must satisfy the requirements set forth in the Assurance Continuity: CCRA Requirements standard.

Major and Minor Releases

Most customers I've encountered realize (or I've made aware) that CC evaluations take a significant amount of time and cost a lot of money. They generally will accept product versions that are "minor releases" of the CC certified version. For example, Symantec Endpoint Security 11.0 (SEP 11.0) received CC certification in June 2008. Customers would be willing to accept SEP 11.1 (if there were such a thing), but not probably not SEP 12.0. The belief is that for "major releases" there would be significant modifications that would impact the security of the product and thus should be re-evaluated.

PART 2: PRE-EVALUATION PREPARATION

In this part:

Chapter 4: Do Your Homework

Conducting background research, gaining stakeholder commitment, and planning are all critical to the successful launch of the evaluation project. To prepare for a CC evaluation, the first thing you should do is to fully understand your customer's requirements. This sounds like a natural thing to do, but I've received frantic phone calls from sales representatives or product managers with no more details about the customer requirements than "we have to get a NIAP certification now or we'll lose a multi-million dollar deal to a competitor." Did the customer require the evaluation against a Protection Profile? If so, which one? What EAL was expected? What product version? These are all important questions to answer before beginning a CC evaluation.

Make it Easy on Yourself

You will need to understand your product and product development, delivery and deployment processes in great detail. Depending on the assurance level (EAL) you are pursuing, you may be required to produce some unusually detailed documentation. I've worked in commercial software product development in Silicon Valley for over 20 years and I know that many of us cut corners when it comes to documenting the details and assumptions about our products and our development processes. CC evaluators sometimes remind me of a new engineer on a project who wants to know how the product works, how it is architected and how it interacts with other parts of the system. S/he will also want to know how to use the source code control system to build and test the code. Product developers don't always make it easy for these newcomers to do their jobs, but in the case of the CC evaluators, if you make their jobs harder, you will pay for it – literally.

Although reading the CC standards documents is a sure cure for insomnia, researching the CC standards [CC Portal] enough to understand what constitutes a security functional requirement (SFR) in CC Part 2 and to be able to connect them with features within your product is important. The CC standards will also reveal what the evaluators have to do meet their requirements and what they will expect in your evidence.

You should also know your product and development processes inside and out as you will need to document these intimate details for the evaluators.

Understand the Customer Requirements

It is insufficient to begin a CC evaluation based on "we need a CC evaluation on product X." If you want to successfully complete your CC evaluation with minimal disruption to your product development team, within your planned timetable and within your prescribed budget, you first must clearly understand what will satisfy your customer. Here are some of the questions I've asked our customers:

- Do they require that the evaluation be performed against a particular Protection Profile (PP)?
- Do they require a specific Evaluation Assurance Level (EAL)?
- What Security Functional Requirements (SFR) do they expect to be included in the evaluation?
- What product version do they expect to be evaluated?
- When do they need the evacuation and certification to be completed?
- Why do they need the product CC evaluated?
- What other (competitor's) products have already been evaluated?
- On what platforms (i.e. operating system or hardware) do they need the evaluation to be performed?

Frankly, most of the responses I've received from customers have been, "huh?" They rarely have any idea what I am talking about and are only trying to meet a general procurement policy requirement. If you are "lucky", the customer will tell you that they want an EAL 4 evaluation with the product version 7.0 running on the Microsoft Vista operating system. If you do get some solid responses from your customer to these questions, you can use this information to frame your evaluation plans. If you get the "huh" response from your customer, you should aim to minimize the evaluation effort (see Chapter 7: Managing Project Scope).

Protection Profile Requirement

Your customer may or may not have stated a Protection Profile requirement, but it is important to know what is out there. A Protection

Profile (PP) is basically a set of CC requirements for a particular product type from the customer's point of view. It contains security functional requirements (SFR) and security assurance requirements (SAR) usually in the form of an EAL. PPs generally are written for a particular type of product such as operating system, database, firewall, intrusion detection systems, or anti-virus. Table 8 lists some of the Protection Profiles that have been formally approved. The current set of approved PPs can be found on the Common Criteria Portal website [CC Portal].

• Anti-Virus	• Certificate Management
• Databases	• Disk Encryption
• Enterprise Security Management	• Firewall
• Intrusion Detection/Prevention System	• Operating System
• Peripheral Switch	• Router
• Security IC Platform (Smart Card)	• USB Encryption
• Virtual Private Network	• Wireless LAN – Client
• Wireless LAN – Access Point	

Table 8: Protection Profiles

Should you choose to consider evaluating your product against the requirements in a Protection Profile (PP), you will need to get the latest version of the PP document and understand the requirements - the SFRs and the EAL requirement. In my experience, I have found that some of our products were covered by an existing Protection Profile (e.g. intrusion detection and anti-virus), but we chose to forgo evaluation against those requirements because the evaluation would take too long and/or the return on investment was not adequate.

Carefully examine each SFR within the applicable PPs. CC Part 2 describes the details of each SFR. I will warn you that some of the terms used in the CC standards have some very specific meanings and you cannot assume that your definition (or even the dictionary definition) of a term is the one used by the evaluator or Scheme. You should be sure that your product performs the necessary functions in the way expected before making claims of meeting the PP requirements; discussing this with your evaluation lab during initial discussions can point out problem areas. Remember, in order to pass an evaluation against a PP, your product must meet 100% of the requirements.

Multi-Function Products

Many IT products these days are "multi-function" and their features may be covered by more than one PP. For example, Symantec Endpoint Protection (SEP) 11.0 includes anti-virus; intrusion detection and prevention; desktop firewall; and content filtering capabilities. Some of these product types are covered by PPs. SEP may be subject to CC evaluations against multiple PPs if a customer decides s/he needs to have all of these functions evaluated. This may prove to be cumbersome if not problematic as not all PPs were written with multi-function products in mind and so there may be conflicting requirements across the various PPs.

The bar chart in Figure 5 created from data collected in April 2010 from the Common Criteria Portal website [CC Portal] illustrates that only a small percentage (8.4%) of the approximately 960 non-smart card products had evaluated against PPs. The breakdown by product type evaluated against PPs is illustrated in the chart. In Chapter 7: Managing Project Scope, I will discuss the issues with PPs and things to think about before deciding to evaluate your product against the PP requirements.

Check the Scheme websites to find out what new PPs are in development and when they will be released. Tracking the requirements within the new PPs can help improve preparation for future evaluations.

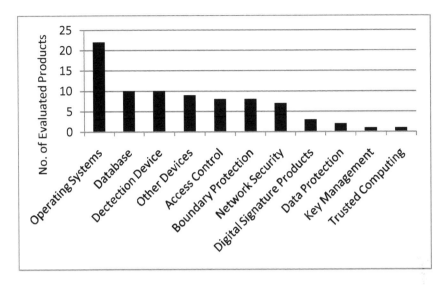

Figure 5: Non-Smart Card Products Evaluated with PPs

Evaluation Assurance Level Requirement

The assurance requirements define the depth and breadth of the evaluation of the secure development, delivery and deployment processes used by the product developer. In this case, depth refers to the amount of evidence produced and reviewed to prove the security claims. Breadth refers to the scope of aspects of the product development processes. For example, EAL 2 does not require any examination of source code or other development security measures but EAL 4 does.

For quite some time, the U.S. government minimum EAL was EAL 2 unless the department or agency procurement policy specified a PP which required a higher EAL. Although the U.S. government typical minimum is EAL 2, some agencies or projects have different standards. You should check with your customers to find out what their EAL expectations are.

CC evaluations up to and including EAL 4 are mutually recognized internationally, so most vendors that intend to sell internationally will evaluate at EAL 2, 3 or 4. CC Part 3 describes the details of the assurance requirements and the *Common Evaluation Methodology* (CEM) provides guidance to the evaluators for each EAL. As a vendor, you should know what the CC evaluators will be expecting and needing in order to complete their tasks. Studying the requirements and instructions in the CC Part 3 and CEM documents will help.

EAL and Security Grades

Sadly, some vendors and customers have been using the EAL as a security "grade" or "score." That is, they have been using the EAL as a competitive differentiator by claiming that a product evaluated at EAL 4 is better or more secure that a product evaluated at EAL 2. While a higher EAL does not mean a product is more secure, the customer perception is that the EAL 4 product is somehow more desirable than an EAL 2 and thus would select the EAL 4 over EAL 2. As a vendor, you can decide to try to use this belief to your advantage or not. In spite of this, I have counseled product teams going through their first CC evaluation to pursue EAL 2 because there is a much greater chance for successful completion than at EAL 4.

The bar graph in Figure 6 was generated from data gathered from the CC Portal website [CC Portal] in April 2010 and illustrates how popular EAL 2 through 4 evaluations were for non-smart card type products. EAL 4 and 5 seemed to be prevalent with smart card products; this is no surprise since most smart card products are evaluated against PPs that require EAL 4 or 5.

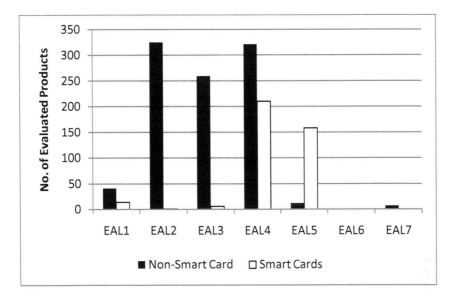

Figure 6: All Evaluated Products By EAL

Security Functional Requirements

Protection Profiles will dictate the SFRs, but even if your customers are not requiring evaluations against PP requirements, they may still have expectations about what SFRs will be included in the evaluation. The selection of SFRs depends largely on what type of product is being evaluated. For example, one would expect that firewalls would have quite a different set of SFRs than a web server.

Product Version Selection

When I've asked sales representatives what version of the product needs to be CC evaluated, the response I usually get is the current shipping product version because generally that is what they are trying to sell to the customer. While I have conducted CC evaluations on current shipping versions in the past, I would recommend that you avoid doing this if at all possible. Since CC evaluations take months or years (depending on product complexity and EAL) to complete and product revisions occur annually or more frequently, by the time you complete a CC evaluation the version you are evaluating may be obsolete. Plan carefully because it is no small feat to switch product versions in the middle of the evaluation process – believe me, I've tried.

Ask the Customer Why

By asking the customer why they need the product to be CC evaluated you can gain some insight into what regulation they are trying to meet. From there, you can do some research into the details of that regulation to further focus your CC evaluation efforts. Some customers may have heard about Common Criteria and understand enough to know that it has something to do with security evaluations. In those rare cases where the customer wants some kind of assurance that the product they are purchasing from you is secure, perhaps a discussion about what secure development measures your teams employ may be sufficient to address their concerns.

Learn About Competitors

I ask customers which competitors already have CC evaluations or have promised to complete them - mostly to gather competitive intelligence, but I also use that information to gain some leverage on the customer who insists that the evaluation be completed before making a purchase decision. I argue that if no other competitors have completed the CC evaluation, then the customer doesn't have much choice but to wait until one of us completes the evaluation. This tactic may buy you some time as you go through your decision making process.

Competition is a strong motivator to pursue CC evaluations. Many customers and sales representatives have told me that we needed to get our products CC evaluated because one of our competitors were in the process or had completed it. Doing more homework in this area helps to determine what your competitive status is and helps frame your plan. If you find that your competitors are also not evaluating their products, you should ask yourself why. You should also determine (along with your product manager) whether there is a competitive advantage to pursing a CC evaluation against a PP or not. The same applies to EAL selection. Customers have been using EAL as the security "grade" for the product. Some think that an EAL 4 is more secure than EAL 2 and thus would prefer to purchase the EAL 4 evaluated product over the EAL 2 evaluated product.

Figure 7 illustrates that the majority of evaluated products historically up to April 2010 according to the Common Criteria Portal data

[CC Portal] were smart card-related devices. These include integrated circuits, various electronic identification cards, and modules. As you can see, after that there is wide variety of products that have been evaluated.

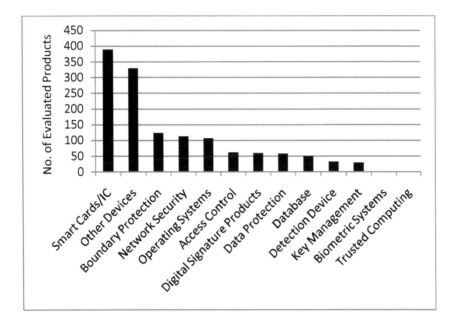

Figure 7: Evaluated Products By Type

Table 9 lists the companies that had the most CC evaluated products [CC Portal] as of April 2010. It includes all product types including smart card devices.

Common Criteria Product Security Evaluations

#	Manufacturer Name	Total Evaluations
1	IBM Corporation	74
2	Infineon Technologies AG	64
3	Konica Minolta Business Technologies, Inc	42
4	Atmel SmartCard ICs	35
5	NXP Semiconductors Germany GmbH	35
6	Fuji Xerox Co., Ltd.	29
7	Philips Semiconductors GmbH	29
8	Microsoft Corporation	27
9	Oracle Corporation	27
10	Samsung Electronics Co., Ltd.	27
11	Cisco Systems	26
12	STMicroelectronics	25
13	T-Systems Enterprise Services GmbH	24
14	OPENLiMiT SignCubes AG	16
15	Giesecke & Devrient GmbH	14
16	Hitachi Ltd.	14
17	Research In Motion	14
18	Sagem Orga GmbH	14
19	Sharp Corporation	14
20	Check Point Software Technologies	13
21	Hewlett-Packard Company	13
22	Secure Computing Corporation	13
23	SymantecCorporation	13
24	Juniper Networks	12
25	McAfee Inc.	12

Table 9: Top Companies

Platforms

CC evaluations are performed on specific platforms. Application software runs on commercial, off-the-shelf hardware and commercial operating systems – these constitute the evaluation platform. The ST identifies the specific set of platforms that are part of the evaluation. The number of platforms can be minimized to make the evaluation project more manageable and to reduce schedule and cost overrun risks. If the customer intends to purchase your product on a specific platform (e.g. Solaris or Windows), then you should be sure to include that platform in your evaluation.

Understand the CC Standards

You will be hiring a CC evaluation lab. You may decide to hire a CC consultant. These people have studied the CC standards and so should you to protect yourself against potential exploitation by these experts. Due diligence dictates that you understand what you are paying for and that you are making the best use of your investments.

Eyes Wide Open

In the first chapters of this book, I have introduced the basic concepts of the CC, the different parts of the CC standards, and an outline of the CC evaluation process. There are a great many details in each of these areas that I will not be able to cover in this book. What I want to emphasize here is that you should engage in the CC evaluation process with your "eyes wide open" - armed with as much information as feasible to help avoid some nasty problems later on.

A Word About CC Training

The intent of this book is to provide useful information to vendors to help them understand all of the important aspects of the CC evaluation process. While I believe this book gives the novice a good start, you may want to hire a consultant or trainer to review and discuss the details and nuances of the CC standards, the evaluation and validation processes, and how all of these relate to the product you plan to have evaluated. You may benefit from having an outside CC expert look at the product you are planning to evaluate to help you decide what path would best suit your needs.

When I first became involved in CC evaluations, I enlisted the help of outside trainers – independent consultants and trainers associated with CC evaluation labs to help our product development teams learn about CC. My experience has shown that customized training for each product development team was the most effective use of their time.

Investigating the specific product security features and connecting those features to CC requirements helped engage the product team members. Also, researching the direct competition and what they have done with CC helped pique interest in learning more.

Over time, I developed and delivered a customized 60 minute training presentation to each product team prior to launching a CC evaluation project with them. I delivered this training to the product manager, program manager (here, the program manager managed the time for all product team members), some key developers, and QA representatives. Here is the outline of the training course that highlights the most important topics to cover as an introduction to the CC evaluation process for product development teams:

1) What is CC?
   a) A standard set of security criteria
   b) A language to describe product security
   c) An evaluation methodology
   d) An international standard (ISO 15408)
   e) Key definitions
      i) Evaluation
      ii) Certification
      iii) Evaluation Assurance Level
      iv) Security Target
      v) Protection Profile
2) Why is it important?
   a) Benefits
   b) Competition
3) How long does it take?
4) How much does it cost?
5) Overall process
   a) Pre-evaluation preparation
   b) Documentation
   c) Roles and responsibilities
   d) Write the Security Target
      i) Define the Target of Evaluation
      ii) Writing the Security Target document
   e) Begin the Evaluation
   f) Create and submit evidence documents
      i) Functional Specifications
      ii) Design
      iii) User Guides

        iv) Test Plans
        v)   Configuration Management procedures
        vi) Delivery, Installation and Setup
        vii) Vulnerability Analysis
    g) Respond to Evaluator Questions
    h) Receive Certificate
    i)   Re-certification
6) Best practices, pitfalls
    a) Meet Minimum Requirements
    b) Allocate Time
    c) Minimize Changes to the Plan
    d) Reuse Certification Materials
    e) Weekly Status Calls with Evaluators
    f)   Dedicated Technical Writer
    g) Synchronize Evaluation with Development
    h) Project Management
7) Product specifics
    a) Potential SFRs
    b) EAL/SAR review against current processes

Common Criteria Portal Website

The Common Criteria standards were developed to be very flexible because it was intended to be used to evaluate the security of a wide variety of IT products. It is also flexible so as to accommodate new, unanticipated technologies that may provide better security. However, with this flexibility comes perhaps some ambiguity and the need to interpret what the authors had intended.

The Common Criteria Portal [CC Portal], the international website for information pertaining to the CC standards, contains not only the standards documents but also documents known as *supporting documents* (SD). SDs augment the CC standards to provide greater guidance to evaluators, validators and product developers and provide a means to attain greater consistency in the evaluation process across the many Schemes and CC evaluation labs. The Smart Card Industry has made great use of supporting documents.

The Common Criteria Portal website [CC Portal] has links to all of the individual national Scheme websites. Many of the National Scheme websites include documents describing their national interpretations and other local publications. The national interpretations and national policy documents are important to vendors as they will dictate specific rules that must be followed in that country.

Common Criteria Vendors' Forum

There is nothing like experience to help you navigate through the complex and confusing CC evaluation process. I have learned a great deal from my experiences with 15 successful and 4 unsuccessful CC evaluations over my 7 years managing these efforts. I have also learned a great deal from talking to my counterparts in other companies. A major reason for the creation of the Common Criteria Vendors' Forum (CCVF) [CCVF] was to provide the connections between vendors to help each other and to share information. I am quite pleased to state that even though many of the members of the CCVF come from competing companies there has been a remarkable amount of information sharing towards addressing common concerns. The CCVF provides a mailing list to post announcements, questions, concerns and comments to fellow members – all of whom are commercial product vendors. As the chair of the CCVF, I have arranged one-on-one conversations with non-competing companies to share best practices and perspectives. The lessons learned from others can help avoid some costly and time-consuming mistakes.

International Common Criteria Conference

The International Common Criteria Conference (ICCC) is another excellent place to meet CC experts. It is a week-long event hosted by a different international CC Mutual Recognition Agreement (CCRA) member's government in the fall each year. This conference includes selected presentations by government representatives, evaluation labs and product vendors. These presentations discuss the latest efforts in CC. There are also status reports from the CC Development Board (CCDB) who sponsor projects to maintain and improve the CC standards and practices. The ICCC attracts all of the experts in CC from around the world. This is an excellent opportunity to meet with influential leaders in this field and to learn more about it from them. CC evaluation labs and consultants also set up booths to market their products and services.

Know Your Product and Processes

How well do you think you know the security attributes of your product and your development processes? I thought I had a good idea before I started my first CC evaluation. CC evaluators need to know what security features are included in your product. When CC evaluators ask about security features, they aren't necessarily asking about how many different viruses your product detects or blocks; they are perhaps more interested in the password strength requirements for an administrator's login and what happens if s/he fails a specified number of login attempts.

CC evaluators also want to know how you securely deliver your product to your end customer. In our case, there are a number of third-parties involved in the delivery process, so no one person can easily answer that question. I had to ask several internal departments including the program manager, someone in IT, and a manufacturing manager along with a couple of external third-parties such as our duplication and distribution partners to definitively answer that question.

Some of the necessary procedures and processes are documented somewhere. Count yourself as one of the lucky ones if you find that documentation and it is up-to-date. Leveraging existing internally-developed documentation is a key factor in the quick start-up of any CC evaluation and is important in successfully completing the project on-time and on-budget. As part of the pre-evaluation preparation, I ask the product development team to gather the following documents:

- Product user manuals
- Product architecture diagram and descriptions
- User-visible error messages
- Test packages
- Product delivery processes
- Defect management processes
- Source code control tools and processes

Naturally, if some of these documents do not exist, you must build into your plan the resources and time to pull together the necessary information and generate these documents.

Over the years and multiple CC evaluations, I developed a pre-evaluation questionnaire that I gave to the product development teams. From their responses, we could determine what additional information we needed to gather and document in preparation for the CC evaluation. The list of questions was not meant to be comprehensive but provided a good first-blush look at how prepared the development team might be for the CC evaluation. Here are some of the questions from that pre-evaluation questionnaire:

Configuration Management
- What documentation do you have on how your team uses configuration management?
- What source code management tools do you use?

Delivery and Operation
- What deviations from the company standard delivery processes do you use with your product?
- Is your product downloadable from the Internet?
- Do you have documentation that describes the "out-of-the-box" product configuration?

Design and Architecture
- Do you have documents or presentations that describe the overall product architecture?
- Do you have a high-level block diagram of the product?
- Do you have any documentation on the major modules in the product that describe their function and interfaces?
- Do you have documentation that describes all of the product's user-viewable error messages?

Guidance Documentation
- Do you have manuals or other instructions that describe administrator functions?
- Do you have manuals or other instructions that describe "normal" user functions?

Testing
- Are most of your tests automated?
- How complex is your test environment to set up?

Vulnerability Analysis
- Are there any reported security vulnerabilities on your product?

- Are there any reported security vulnerabilities on any third-party component that you product uses?

Product Features
- What (security or administrative) events does your product log?
- What kind of data is recorded in the logs?
- How do users view the audit logs?
- Are user name and password required to access the product features?
- Do you have documentation that describes what kind of configuration settings users can set?
- What kind of user roles does the product support?

Chapter 5: Developing the Business Case

Obtaining executive approval for the large investment of time and money required for CC evaluations is critical to being able to start (and sustain) the evaluation project. One of the greatest challenges I've faced in preparing for a CC evaluation was developing a convincing and compelling business case. Sometimes the business executives and product team members immediately recognized the importance of meeting this requirement and were willing to devote their resources to it. In those cases, I suspect that the customer had either taken their case directly to the executives recently or the competition had threatened to lock them out of some large sales opportunities. In most cases, however a business case had to be developed to convince the business leaders to proceed.

There are obviously two major components to developing a return-on-investment (ROI) business case to pursue a CC evaluation. They are:

1. Costs (investments)
2. Benefits (returns)

Costs of CC Evaluations

Among the first questions that development managers ask me when they first encounter a CC evaluation are how much will it cost and how long will it take? Both of these questions need to be answered in order to complete your business case and before you can decide whether you can go forward with the CC evaluation.

Understanding how much the CC evaluation will cost requires that you have done your homework to understand the requirements, your product capabilities, and the evidence gaps. You also need to account for all of the costs to meet the requirements. Here are the major cost (i.e. money expense) categories:

1. CC consultant or in-house evidence development costs
2. Evaluation lab costs
3. Travel expenses for consultants and evaluation lab personnel
4. Validator fees (if any from the selected national Scheme)
5. Equipment costs for any special test set-ups

CC evaluations are costly. I managed to get the cost of an EAL 2 evaluation down to $340,000 including: the cost of a CC consultant to write our evidence documentation, evaluation lab fees, and travel expenses. This was for a relatively simple product with a minimal set of evaluated security functions. Because the financial outlays for a CC evaluation can be significant, everyone wants to know how much they have to pay. Based on some of my experiences here are some example cost breakdowns:

EAL 2 Estimates
- $170,000 in CC consulting for evidence production
- $170,000 in CC evaluation lab fees

EAL 4 Estimates
- $500,000 in consulting and evaluation lab fees

These figures are based on a compilation of several products. The disclaimer is that no two products are alike and no two product development teams are alike, so there can be wide variation in the actual costs with any CC evaluation.

In 2004, the NIAP director [Dale] reported the following evaluation cost estimates shown in Table 10. NIAP collected this information from several U.S. CC evaluation labs.

EAL Level	Evaluation Costs
EAL 2	$100,000 – $170,000
EAL 3	$130,000 – $225,000
"Simple" EAL 4	$175,000 - $300,000
"Complex" EAL 4	$300,000 - $750,000

Table 10: Cost Estimates from NIAP

An associated cost to the evaluation lab fees are travel expenses. Most evaluation labs will break out their travel expenses separately from the evaluation lab fees. With most CC evaluations, a site visit is required. This means the evaluation lab personnel must come to your development site(s) and observe your operations. At EAL 2, they will want to see how developers actually use the source code configuration management systems. They will also want to see the product ordering and delivery systems. They are there to confirm that the procedures you have documented in your configuration management and delivery documentation accurately portray reality.

Site Visit Expenses

One of our products was delivered on an original equipment manufacturer (OEM) hardware box, so the evaluators felt it necessary to visit our out-of-state OEM hardware manufacturer to observe their operations. Travel expenses included airfare, rental cars, hotel and meals. In some instances, I have been charged for the evaluator's time on an hourly basis during the site visit. It is important to budget for site visit costs since it can last a few days to a week resulting in a significant cost.

Some national CC Schemes charge vendors a fee to cover their validation costs. Validators oversee the work of the evaluation labs to ensure consistent evaluations across the country and the world. Some Schemes base their fees on the EAL. The higher the EAL, the more effort and time they have to put in, so the more they charge. Other Schemes will charge a flat fee. These fees need to be understood and then factored into your CC evaluation budget.

In CC evaluations we did in the U.K., the U.K. Scheme [CESG] charged fees of up to $30,000 for an EAL 4 evaluation. The U.K. Scheme charges validation fees according to the complexity of the product and evaluation – basically to cover the costs of the validator to review the work.

The German Scheme (BSI) charges validation fees for CC evaluations performed in their country. Fees are based on product complexity and EAL. According to information on the BSI website [BSI], fees range from 2,500 Euro for a simple product (e.g. smart card) at EAL 2 to 9,000 Euro for a complex product (e.g. operating system) at EAL 4.

The Australasian Scheme (AISEP) [Australasia] Program Policy dated 26 September 2006 listed certification fees ranging from 5,500 Australian dollars for EAL 1 up to 33,000 Australian dollars for EAL 7.

Finally, an expense that surprised me while in the middle of an evaluation was equipment costs. The evaluation lab is obligated to order, install and test the actual product as part of the evaluation. While ordering a "not-for-resale" (NFR) product didn't cost us anything in most cases, any special or additional hardware the evaluation lab needed to assemble the evaluated configuration had to be purchased. Special equipment may be OEM appliances, routers, specialized servers or disk drives. Most evaluation labs are well-equipped with standard computer and networking hardware in sufficient supply so as to accommodate the many projects they may be performing simultaneously, but any unusual equipment needs to be purchased for their use.

Ordering and delivering hardware can take time and may impact the evaluation schedule. As part of the scheduling exercise, be sure to account for any necessary lead time for ordering and delivery to the evaluation lab.

Since time is money, stakeholders are concerned about how much time it will take to complete a CC evaluation. The best case scenario I have experienced was with an EAL 2 evaluation of a simple product; it took 10 months total. Table 11 shows estimates gathered by NIAP from various U.S. labs in 2004 [Dale]. The NIAP estimates may not include initial contract set up time and validation time which would account for the differences from my estimates.

EAL Level	Evaluation Times
EAL 2	4 - 6 months
EAL 3	6 - 9 months
"Simple" EAL 4	7 - 12 months
"Complex" EAL 4	12 - 24 months

Table 11: Time Estimates from NIAP

Lost opportunity costs must also be factored into the decision-making process to proceed with a CC evaluation. Every minute a development engineer has to spend pulling together information for the evaluation evidence or answering questions from the evaluation lab is time away from his/her main job of creating value-added functions for an up-coming product release. This may equate to lost competitive advantage and lost sales revenue to commercial enterprises. My experience has shown that for an EAL 2, the development team can expect to expend 250 person-hours answering questions and gathering information for the consultant and evaluation lab. For EAL 4 evaluations my estimate is 500 person-hours.

Time-to-market (TTM) can also be affected by interrupting the development team for a CC evaluation. TTM or beating the competition to the marketplace with a new feature can have a significant impact on long-term revenues. There have been several studies done to illustrate how TTM impacts revenue; basically, the leader gains the lion's share of market share in many instances.

$$\text{Total Costs} \quad = \quad \left[\begin{array}{l} \text{Evaluation Lab costs +} \\ \text{CC consultant costs +} \\ \text{Other expenses +} \\ \text{Validator Fees +} \\ \text{Equipment Costs +} \\ \text{Lost Opportunity Costs} \end{array} \right.$$

Figure 8: Total Cost Components

Figure 8 summarizes all the cost components to consider for CC evaluations. Now, let's examine how these costs can be offset by the benefits.

Benefits of CC Evaluations

To complete the ROI analysis, you will need to understand and quantify the benefits of CC evaluation. Basically, what are the expected returns on your investment? In my experience, it has been very difficult to quantify the incremental revenue and other benefits of CC evaluations. In many cases, we have proceeded with CC evaluations simply because the product manager felt threatened by competitors who had completed CC evaluations or had announced plans to do it – fear is a strong motivator.

I have had a difficult time finding solid data to support any quantitative analysis for a variety of reasons. Usually, the CC evaluation issue comes up when a government agency's license contract comes up for renewal and they have to demonstrate compliance to the government procurement policy requirements. At that point, there is no upside revenue potential, only the risk of losing the renewal. In the cases where a new customer is seeking a CC evaluated solution, the contract amount is apparent. These new, multi-million dollar opportunities often attract management attention and support.

The trick is to develop arguments (quantitative or not) that will support the claims for business benefits to your company. I have researched the CC evaluation status of competitors to highlight our potential competitive weaknesses if we did not pursue CC evaluations. I have also gathered historical data on lost deals to competitors who had CC evaluated products. I have projected incremental revenues based on the pipeline of upcoming contracts from the government that would require CC evaluated products. I've found that different approaches and different arguments work with different managers. Perhaps the key to success here is to learn what kinds of arguments are most persuasive for the managers you have to convince. Some key considerations for developing your business case are:

1. What happens if you do proceed?
2. What happens if you don't?
3. What happens if you do it later?

Not only should you consider the ROI of proceeding with the CC evaluation but you should also consider the ROI if you do not. This refers to the notion of lost opportunity costs – what opportunities would you be missing if you spent time on the CC evaluation?

Another key consideration is what happens if you defer your decision? If you defer, what are the positive and negative impacts? I have found that sometimes waiting helps clarify the needs and opportunities. An important consideration here is the fact that even though you complete a CC evaluation, you can still lose the contract to a competitor for other reasons.

Return on Investment

Return on investment is simply the potential returns minus the costs of proceeding with a CC evaluation divided by the costs.

$$ROI = (Benefits - Costs) / Costs$$

Figure 9: Definition of ROI

If the ROI is significant enough, proceeding with the CC evaluation makes good business sense. You should note that just because the ROI is non-negative does not necessarily mean it is the right thing to do. Most companies have a threshold or target return on their investments. Without going into MBA-like details, most companies are looking for a certain percentage return on any investment. Many Silicon Valley firms are looking for returns on their R&D investments of 100 to 1,000 fold.

That is, for every $1 they invest in R&D, they expect a return of $100 or $1,000 in additional revenue. So, for a $300,000 investment in an EAL 2 CC evaluation, a normal expected return might be $30M in incremental revenue. That may be a tough argument to justify!

Table 12 illustrates an example ROI analysis accounting for all of the costs and benefits. Whether the 10.36 return on investment in the example is sufficient to justify the investment is a business judgment call.

COSTS	
CC Consultant	
Evidence development	$ 160,000
Travel and Expenses	$ 10,000
CC Evaluation Lab	
Evaluation costs	$ 155,000
Travel and Expenses	$ 15,000
Equipment costs	$ 5,000
Validators	
Validation fees	$ 20,000
Lost opportunities	
Lost opportunity costs	$ 1,000,000
Total Costs	**$ 1,365,000**
RETURNS	
Revenue preserved	$ 10,000,000
Incremental revenue	$ 5,000,000
Leveraged sales	$ 500,000
Total Returns	**$ 15,500,000**
ROI	10.36

Table 12: ROI Example

Intangibles

I have found that even though commercial vendors and their leaders seem to want to make analytical decisions about most things there have been occasions where quantitative, analytical return-on-investment business cases are not effective in convincing executives. Sometimes a more qualitative or strategic approach is more effective. This may depend on the personality of the decision-makers or some other factors.

I have found that one of the strongest motivators for CC evaluations is the threat of losing competitive advantage to a rival company product. I found this influence the strongest when the competition was head-to-head. For example, Symantec's Enterprise Firewall product faced stiff competition from Cisco's PIX Firewall especially in the government sector. Cisco's products and their PIX firewall had been involved with CC evaluations from the beginning; this proved to be a strong motivator for the product team to attain parity from the CC evaluation perspective.

For awhile I thought I could develop an argument that commercial enterprise sales were influenced by government sales. That is, if the government bought a CC evaluated product, the commercial enterprises would take notice and be inclined to follow the government's lead. If that were true, then perhaps the commercial enterprises would also recognize CC evaluations as an important purchasing factor since the government did. In my research, I found a few commercial enterprise customers who had heard of the Common Criteria but none who actually required CC evaluated products. Although accounting for increased sales from non-government sectors for CC evaluated products sounded good in theory, I have not been able to prove a correlation here.

I also thought that I could develop arguments that the government was a strategic market and CC evaluations are a long-term investment, thus reducing the need for a short-term ROI justification. I think depending on your company's strategic planning process and the view of what businesses and markets your company deems are strategic will determine how successfully you can argue this point.

One reason we need a strong business case is to convince an executive champion to allocate the necessary resources. In the next chapter, I will discuss resource allocations for the CC evaluation project to determine who does what.

Chapter 6: Resource Allocation

Proper resource allocation for your CC evaluation project is critical to its successful completion. Several CC evaluation projects I was involved in failed to complete because the appropriate resources were not committed to the project. Later in this book (Chapter 14: Success Stories), I will discuss the need for adhering to the good project management practice of monitoring and controlling including ensuring that project resources are applied when needed, but this chapter will focus on initial resource allocation planning.

Who Does What?

To fully understand the CC evaluation process, you should understand the roles and responsibilities of all of the parties involved including:

- Developers and QA team members
- CC consultants
- CC evaluation lab
- Validators
- Executive champion

Developers and QA

The product developers and quality assurance (QA) members are the product technical experts. They are expected to understand how the product was put together, how it was tested, and what features it has. This technical information is the core of the CC evaluation – examining the product from the security point of view. Within these individual's brains lay the details necessary to complete the CC evaluation. Unless there are complete, accurate and up-to-date documents that can adequately explain all of the security details the CC evaluator will need, the technical team will be called upon to answer questions and provide input. Recognizing that developer time is limited by other product release demands, planning their time carefully becomes imperative.

Product developers, including QA and product management, provide the technical details about the product and the product development processes. It helps to have a product architecture block diagram including all of the major components as a reference. Test plans, test scripts, expected and actual test results are generally required for any CC evaluation. The evaluators will want to review configuration management and vulnerability remediation processes. Throughout the process, the product developers must be readily available to answer questions from the CC evaluation lab. Any delays in responses to these inquiries will affect the scheduled completion of the evaluation.

CC Consultants

External third-party CC consultants or internal technical writers are needed to augment or adapt the existing technical documents for submission as evidence to the CC evaluators. Some say that CC evaluations are nothing but a paper exercise and most labs spend the majority of their time reviewing documents rather than actually testing the products - the CC standards dictate this so providing complete and accurate evidence documents to the evaluators is critical.

CC consultants or internal technical writers are responsible for creating any CC evidence documentation that doesn't already exist. Consultants may also take existing internal documentation and customize it for the evaluators. The CC consultant also needs to be responsive to questions and comments from the evaluators. A good consultant who understands the product and the development processes will be able to address most of the comments from the evaluation lab without having to bother the development team.

CC Evaluation Lab

The CC evaluation lab is responsible for fulfilling the requirements described in the *Common Evaluation Methodology* (CEM). They will be responsible for evaluating evidence documentation, conducting any necessary vendor site visits, providing feedback and questions to the vendor, producing evaluation reports, and responding to comments from the Scheme validators.

Validators

The national Scheme validators are government employees or government contractors who oversee the evaluation work of the evaluation lab. They ensure that the evaluation reports are complete and consistent with the standards. The Scheme issues the official certificate to the vendor upon completion of the evaluation and validation phases. Practically speaking, Schemes may on occasion interact directly with the vendors to improve their understanding of the security of the product; however, in most cases it is the responsibility of the evaluation lab to respond to Scheme inquiries.

Executive Champion

An executive sponsor or champion will help promote and defend the CC evaluation project from the outset on through to completion. Even if you develop a solid business case to initiate the project, as time passes, business conditions change and priorities may shift. When that happens, it helps to have an executive sponsor who will continue to defend the CC evaluation projects. Our public sector sales vice president was an effective supporter for these evaluations; on some occasions the product's business unit leader was our champion.

Points of Contact

Perhaps the most important people in CC evaluations are the points of contact (POC) for each party involved. There invariably are going to be problems that need to be addressed – some may require immediate attention. Having a single point of contact that is responsible for coordinating with others on their "side" to address issues helps ensure a successful CC evaluation project. In my experience, we had many occasions where we had to contact the various POCs to address technical questions or expedite delivery of documents.

Project Manager

The project manager is responsible for maintaining the overall project schedule. S/he will communicate on a regular basis with the CC consultant, evaluation lab and development team to make sure they are on schedule and to manage around any deviations. As with any project manager, s/he is responsible for planning, monitoring and controlling the process.

Product Manager

Every product has a product manager – someone who will communicate with customers and the sales representatives about the latest product features and plans. CC evaluations can be used as a competitive differentiator; promoting them can influence customers' buying decisions. Keeping the product manager informed of the evaluation progress so that s/he can inform customers will help position the product in a competitive environment. In my role, I served as the product manager for product certifications, so I took on the responsibility for educating customers and sales representatives on our CC evaluation plans and status.

Time Investments

Resource allocation is always a challenge especially when long, expensive endeavors such as CC evaluations come up unexpectedly. Try as we might, we always seemed to have a difficult time developing a long-term roadmap of CC evaluations. We would too often be confronted with customer "opportunities" that required products to undergo CC evaluations in short timeframes. Resources, including people, time and money have to be allocated to CC evaluations in order to ensure success. Here are some frequently asked questions that come up during the planning stages:

- Where is time spent?
- How much time is spent?

Where Is Time Spent?

In our 15 successful CC product evaluations, the bulk of the time spent by the development and QA team members was in the following areas:

1. Assembling the raw technical information
2. Formatting documentation for the CC evaluators
3. Developing special test cases
4. Responding to CC evaluator's questions

Much to the chagrin of security professionals, most product development teams do not readily have information about the security of their products much less have any documentation about it. In order to answer questions like: "How does this security feature work?" or "How do you securely deliver your product?" the developers have to spend time investigating and researching. Some questions are easy to answer if you can find the person that actually implemented the code that executes the security function in question; it becomes much more difficult when that person is no longer with the company and there is no documentation available.

I found that the product delivery process involves many internal departments and several third-parties. To fully describe the security of our delivery process involved discussions with each department - understanding the interfaces between them and even examining the systems they each used. Fortunately, all of our products used the same delivery processes, so I only had to go through that effort once.

The job of the CC consultant is to develop the evidence for the CC evaluators. The value the CC consultant brings is his/her knowledge of how to convey the right information to the CC evaluator such as to minimize further questions and save time. Formatting the evidence documentation so that the CC evaluators can quickly extract the information they need to complete their requirements for CEM is an art form. I have found that CC evaluators want simple, clean and consistent descriptions. A really good CC consultant will minimize the number of rework loops with the evaluator. However, to accomplish this takes time. If you choose not to use an experienced CC consultant to develop the evidence documentation, be prepared to get a lot of "feedback" from the evaluators.

At most assurance levels (EAL), the CC evaluation lab must examine the security testing plans and results. Since many of our product development teams did not do much security-specific testing, we had to develop some special test plans and test scripts just for the CC evaluation. For example, each of our products required the administrative user to login to the system with a user name and password. The testing of such a feature usually consisted of a single, valid user name and password to start a session. The normal test suite did not include any abuse cases or any attempts to circumvent the identification and authentication mechanisms of the product. In order to satisfy the CC evaluator's examination of this function, we had to develop test cases that tried to break the security feature. Depending on your product test methodology and the amount of test automation you use will determine how much time it will take to develop and run these CC-specific tests for your product.

Make it Easy for the Evaluators

I have encountered some CC evaluators who were "picky"; some returned evidence because of typographical errors or slightly inconsistent use of terminology. At the time, I was extremely annoyed at these comments because we were paying the evaluation lab and the consultant on a time-and-materials basis, so each rework loop was costing us money. The lesson here is that your (and your CC consultant's) job is to make the CC evaluator's job easy.

My opinion is that the CC paradigm was established to make the job of the evaluator as easy as possible. The CC was formed partly to increase the scale and reach of evaluated products. With ITSEC and the *Orange Book*, only government experts conducted product security evaluations. With the CC, non-government entities were enlisted to perform evaluations. Commercial labs were established and accredited to serve these needs. As a result of increasing the scale, the evaluation methodology had to be exercisable by a wider population. This meant pushing the responsibility of making the evidence more consumable down to the product vendor.

In addition to the initial collection of technical information about the product and the secure development processes, developers will spend time answering questions from the CC evaluators. In most cases, once the evaluation has begun and the CC consultants have gathered all of the preliminary information they need to generate the evidence documents, developers spend little time answering questions. The issue becomes a matter of timing. Developers often have to juggle conflicting priorities - their time is valuable. Often developers are pulled away from projects to deal with "hot" issues. So while questions from CC evaluators may not take much time to answer, developers may just simply not be available to answer them. I have also encountered situations where questions from CC evaluators required developers to spend time doing research and investigation (i.e. digging through source code) to find the answers. Some of the most significant delays came in cases where internal documentation was lacking and the authors were no longer with the company.

How Much Time is Spent?

A natural question every product development team that is about to embark on a CC evaluation asks is: "How much time is spent on this?" There are of course no really good ways to estimate this, but based on my experiences here are some numbers to use as a starting point for discussion.

Depending on the complexity of your product, expect developers to spend 20 person-hours total gathering technical information for the CC consultant to write the Security Target document. I am assuming here that there are some internal documents and customer manuals to leverage. It can take 2 calendar-months to write a solid Security Target document, so expect the developers to be engaged on-and-off during that time period.

Once the evaluation process has begun, developers can spend 2 hours per week assembling data and responding to questions from the CC consultant and the evaluators. I have found that developers can spend much more time at this if there is little or no internal documentation from which to draw. For planning purposes, allocating 2 hours per week for the entire duration of the CC evaluation is a good rule of thumb.

The amount of effort spent developing special tests for the CC evaluations depends largely on the amount of automation and tools used by the QA staff. Reducing the scope of the evaluation will help minimize the impact of this effort.

I highly recommend weekly status calls with the CC consultant and evaluators to assess project status and discuss any issues. Project managers will recognize that for any project, monitoring the status and immediately addressing any issues will help lead to a successful project. These meetings were usually 30 minute teleconferences including the points of contact for each party involved.

Table 13 summarizes a sample time allocation for the key players at each phase of the evaluation.

Personnel	Pre-Evaluation	Evaluation	Validation
Developers / QA	20 person-hours	2 person-hours/week	
	Gather technical information	Answer questions Develop tests	Wait
Project manager	3 person-hours / week	1 person-hour / week	
	Planning, monitoring, controlling	Monitoring	
Product manager	5 person-hours	1 person-hour / week	2 person-hours / week
	Gather product information	Attend status meetings	Advertise certification

Table 13: Example Time Allocations

Develop a Preliminary Evaluation Work Plan and Schedule

If this is your first CC evaluation, I would suggest enlisting the help of a CC consultant or perhaps a CC evaluation lab to map out the preliminary work plan and schedule. You will have to engage the evaluation lab before you can officially be *In Evaluation* anyway, so it wouldn't hurt to engage them in your initial planning stages. The important thing to coordinate with the CC evaluation lab is when the various evidence documents will be delivered for evaluation. There seems to be a "natural" order for evaluating the different documents, but you should coordinate this with your CC evaluation lab. The "normal" order of deliverables, I've experienced is:

1. Security Target
2. Configuration management
3. Delivery, installation and operation
4. User guidance
5. Lifecycle support
6. Development including functional specifications, design and architecture
7. Tests
8. Vulnerability analysis

Chapter 6: Resource Allocation

From an initial planning perspective, the CC evaluation project is like every other project where you need to estimate who will be doing what by when. You need to be clear on what deliverables will be produced and exchanged between the various parties. A Gantt chart of activities developed during the initial planning process is a useful tool.

Planning, including resource allocation, is an important responsibility of the project manager. Resource allocation is critical to developing a solid business case and to gain commitment from the developers, QA, business leaders and other internal stakeholders. Having a solid plan from the outset addresses many of the common questions and helps to build credibility that the project will be successful and lead to improved business results.

Chapter 7: Managing Project Scope

Whether you think Common Criteria (CC) evaluations are "just a government procurement checkbox" or whether it is a step along the road to more secure products, you have a corporate obligation to try to minimize costs while increasing benefits ("get more bang for your buck"). Because CC evaluations are such large projects, costs are scrutinized and cost overruns are frowned upon. It becomes important that the CC project manager carefully plan, monitor and control the project costs throughout the life of the project.

In the case of CC evaluations, time IS money. Many evaluation labs and CC consultants charge on a time and materials (T&M) basis, so the more time they spend on reworking or re-assessing documents, the more money you have to spend to complete the evaluation. I will discuss lab and consultant contracts in more detail in Chapter 8: Partner Selection. With CC evaluations, the vendor pays for everything including:

- Evaluation lab fees
- Validator time (in some countries)
- Consultants (or technical writers)

Another major reason for minimizing the time for CC evaluations is that the longer an evaluation takes, the greater the risk that the evaluation will never be completed. Products may change significantly during the course of the evaluation (which can take months or years). These product changes may invalidate the evidence and can adversely impact the CC evaluation process to the point that the evaluation has to be completely restarted. On top of that, the U.S. Scheme, NIAP [NIAP], has issued some policy letters stating that they are imposing time limits on evaluations.

> ### Quick and Cheap
>
> My approach to CC was to complete the CC evaluations as quickly as possible. Since CC evaluations did not have any significant impact on improving product security and was viewed primarily as a procurement requirement, satisfying the checkbox requirement as quickly and cheaply as possible was the objective.
>
> I have experienced a couple of CC evaluations that took so long that the version we started evaluating was obsolesced by a newer version. We had to update all of the CC evidence documents to reflect the changes to the product. These changes meant we had to pay the writer to make the modifications and pay the CC evaluation lab to re-evaluate the changes. This of course led to further time delays.

Here are three best practices related to managing project scope that I've discovered during my experience with CC evaluations:

1. Meet minimum requirements
2. Minimize changes to the plan
3. Leverage evidence

Meet Minimum Requirements

Since time is money, it is important to reduce time risks from you evaluation projects to minimize costs and improve the return on investment. I have successfully driven time risk out of my CC evaluation projects by reducing the scope of the evaluations. You can reduce the scope of the evaluation by following these steps:

- Assess Customer Minimum Requirements
- Avoid Protection Profiles
- Minimize the TOE Scope
- Minimize System Configurations
- Minimize EAL Claims
- Avoid Misusing CC Evaluations

Assess Customer Minimum Requirements

Many of my customers simply say they require that our products have a CC evaluation. Some will quote the U.S. Department of Defense procurement policy, NSTISSP #11 [NSTISSP], and say the intrusion detection (IDS) product must be evaluated against the U.S. government-approved IDS Protection Profiles (PP). Others will say we have to do an EAL 4 evaluation because that is their agency's standard. Whatever the stated customer requirements are, do your homework and truly understand what these requirements mean to your product and your development organization. For some development organizations, EAL 4 is not possible without some changes in the way they produce their products. Meeting some of the esoteric requirements in the U.S. government-approved PPs may require significant product re-engineering. It is imperative that you fully understand what the EAL and PP requirements are and what impact they have on your evaluation effort.

I would recommend that when you are faced with some customer requirements that may require significant effort to meet, that you analyze the various options and their respective benefits. For example, one of the U.S. Army's requirements was that our IDS product needed to be CC evaluated against the IDS PP for *medium robustness environments* (MRE). Simply put, MRE required CC evaluations at a level greater than EAL 4. Evaluations at that level are extremely time-consuming and are not internationally recognized. Meanwhile there were other customers who required only EAL 2 evaluations for that same product. Given that this was the first CC evaluation for this product and this development team, the decision was made to first complete an EAL 2 evaluation, examine the incremental revenue benefits and then revisit the Army's requirement for medium robustness. The lower assurance evaluation minimized the scope of the effort and time, increased the chance of success and met the requirements for some customers. My concern was that if we embarked upon trying to meet the Army's requirements first, that we would never finish and we would meet none of our customers' CC evaluation requirements.

Avoid Protection Profiles

In the U.S., for many years, NIAP has upheld the policy stated in NSTISSP #11 [NSTISSP] and DODI 8500.2. DODI 8500.2 dated February 6, 2003 stated that:

- If a Protection Profile (PP) for a given product type exists and products have been validated against the PP, then DOD agencies must procure only those validated products
- If a PP for a given product type exists but no products have been validated against the PP, then vendors are required to submit their products for evaluation and validation against the applicable PP in order to be considered for DOD procurement
- If no PP exists for the given product type, then the vendor must submit their products for evaluation and validation against the vendor-provided Security Target (ST)

Figure 10 illustrates the decision process described in the DOD instructions.

In spite of the DOD policy notice, individual DOD agencies and projects seemed to disregard it and did not require CC evaluations against the applicable PPs. Given the confusion and inconsistency of the behavior of the government customers, vendors should exercise good business judgment to drive decisions to pursue CC evaluations against PPs.

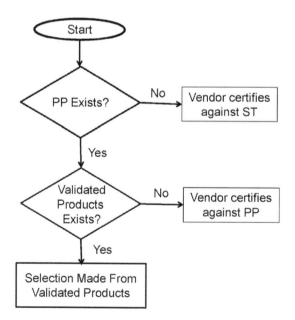

Figure 10: PP Decision Tree

One big reason why I feel that product development teams will have a difficult time meeting the requirements in a PP on their first CC evaluation is that I have little faith in the practicality of some of the PPs that exist today; the exceptions may be the set of PPs for smart cards. My past experience with PP authors has been less than impressive. I recall having a discussion with the authors of the IDS PP several years ago. They wanted to include a requirement that all alerts from the IDS should not only be displayed on the administrator's console, but that they were not to "scroll off" the screen until the administrator acknowledged the alert. This remark rekindled an old memory of mine when I was working on a DEC PDP-11 and a teletype console in the 1980s. I told them that 1) IDS's can generate hundreds of alerts per minute and it would be impractical to expect the human administrator to acknowledge each one in real-time and 2) alerts don't scroll off the teletype anymore – that is an implementation- or technology-specific requirement and should not be in a PP. I had a similar incident with the authors of the anti-virus PP years later.

Minimize The TOE Scope

A major effort to manage the project scope and a part of the pre-evaluation assessment is the definition of the *Target of Evaluation* (TOE). In most cases, the TOE is a subset of functionality of the product you want to have evaluated. This subset becomes apparent when you are asked to describe the *TOE boundary* in the *Security Target* (ST) document. The ST summarizes what is being evaluated and to what depth (EAL). The TOE is illustrated usually with a diagram and descriptive text. The major components or building blocks of the TOE are shown and described. A dotted line around the TOE is an effective way to define the *TOE boundary* to show what parts of the product are being evaluated and what parts of the product are being excluded.

I say the TOE is usually a subset of the product because many of the products I have been involved with include features such as auto-update which includes a connection to corporate back office systems that push product updates to customers. While this capability is part of every product, it would be impractical to submit our back office systems into the CC evaluation. We exclude these capabilities from the TOE for simplicity.

> ## Third-Party Code
>
> I am reminded by some evaluators that third-party and open source code (basically code you don't own such as databases, web servers and cryptographic libraries) can be included in the TOE and treated as subsystems. At EAL 1 through 3, only external interface descriptions are required, so there is no need to obtain detailed internal design or implementation information about the module for the evaluation. For EAL 4 (ADV_TDS.3) and higher, you will be required to produce more detailed descriptions of the internals of that third-party code.

I have had several arguments with product managers who want to somehow market product features through CC evaluations. They want to include product features that may be unique and are marketed to our customers as differentiators but are not appropriate for CC evaluations. These irrelevant features add time, cost and risk to the evaluation project. Some product managers may be under the impression that customers are going to read the ST, review the certification report, and somehow see that the marketable features were CC evaluated; then upon realizing that the feature was CC-certified, decide to buy the product. This scenario is pure fantasy. Customers rarely read the ST and even if they could, the marketable feature would be buried beneath CC jargon so as to be indistinguishable.

Distributed development is a business reality today but to reduce the need for the CC evaluator to go on multiple site visits, ensure that each site uses the same development practices and that you have sufficient documentation to prove it.

Minimize System Configurations

A factor to consider is the complexity of the system configuration. CC evaluation labs must install, set up and test the TOE usually in their own lab. In order to reduce the time to setup and test the TOE in the proper configuration, you should simplify the system configuration as much as possible while attempting to simulate a reasonable customer environment. For example, many products have the option of deploying administrator consoles to be run remotely or to be run co-resident with the server computer. To reduce the complexity of the setup and remove the need to configure a specialized network, consider using the co-resident configuration for the evaluation.

Also consider what platforms to use in the evaluation. All CC evaluations must select hardware and operating system platforms upon which the evaluation will be performed. Technically, the evaluation is only valid on those tested platforms. For example, the Symantec Endpoint Protection product is supported on a variety of operating systems including Microsoft Windows Vista, Windows XP and several Windows Server platforms. Each platform represents additional evaluation and testing work and increases costs and time to complete the evaluation. In the CC evaluations I've led, we have selected the most popular platform(s) as the basis of the evaluation. On occasion, we will get customers who actually look closely enough at the CC certificate to check that the operating system they will be using was part of the evaluation; however most don't check.

Applications and Platforms

As an application software developer, I take issue with the claim that CC evaluations are about just the TOE and yet the evaluations must specify what hardware and operating system platforms are part of the evaluated configurations. The TOEs I've dealt with are application software products running on commercial standard operating systems and commercial hardware. I have no control over the security of these operating systems. If I am evaluating the application software, why should I have to worry about the platforms? If the operating system (OS) is insecure, then the OS should be evaluated by the OS vendor. In my mind, this is where CC evaluations cross the line into system and environment certification.

Minimize EAL Claims

In order to properly manage the scope of your product evaluation, you should understand what is required to meet the requirements the different EALs. Most commercial products are evaluated at EAL 2 – 4. What are the real differences between these EALs? EAL 2 is the minimum assurance level allowed by the U.S. government agencies and in my opinion, the lowest level that provides any customer value. I believe that most relatively mature product organizations are capable of meeting the requirements in EAL 2, but I have heard from evaluators that some product developers perhaps are not quite so mature and have had difficulty meeting the EAL 2 requirements. Here are the assurance requirements for EAL 2:

EAL 2 Requirements

Development
- ADV_ARC.1 - Security architecture description
- ADV_FSP.2 - Security-enforcing functional specification
- ADV_TDS.1 - Basic design

EAL 2 requires a high-level description of the product's security architecture – how security features cannot be bypassed, how it protects itself from tampering, and how installation is secure. If you haven't given any thought to how your product does these things, you will need to and then document it. This requirement is the same through EAL 4.

Functional specifications at EAL 2 must describe all of the security functions, their interfaces and error messages. Once you have decided what security functions you will include in the evaluation, it should not take too much effort to describe these functions. I have found though that finding the error messages that each generates takes some effort.

TOE design is required at EAL 2 in addition to the security architecture; you will be required to describe the TOE in terms of subsystems, their interfaces, and their security-enforcing behaviors. I have found that a block diagram depicting these subsystems to be a helpful tool to meet this requirement.

Guidance Documents
- AGD_OPE.1 - Operational user guidance
- AGD_PRE.1 - Preparative procedures

The guidance requirements at EAL 2 are the same through EAL 4. Operational and preparative guidance give the customer instructions on how to securely install, configure and operate the TOE. These instructions must directly reflect the security functions included in the Security Target. Insecure installation and configuration issues have been reported as a major source of system vulnerabilities by SANS and OWASP [OWASP].

Lifecycle Support
- ALC_CMC.2 - Production support, acceptance procedures and automation
- ALC_CMS.2 - Problem tracking CM coverage
- ALC_DEL.1 - Delivery procedures

Lifecycle support requirements at EAL 2 focus on configuration management and secure delivery processes. Be prepared to document the configuration management (i.e. source code control) system you use and how access to the TOE and all of its components are securely managed. Similarly, you will also be required to describe the end-to-end delivery processes and how the security of the TOE is maintained. You should consider how anyone might maliciously or accidentally tamper with the product during delivery to your customers and how your systems and procedures counter such tampering.

Tests
- ATE_COV.1 - Evidence of coverage
- ATE_FUN.1 - Functional testing
- ATE_IND.2 - Independent testing - simple

Testing at EAL 2 is a combination of vendor testing coverage and independent testing performed by the evaluation lab. As the vendor, you have only a little input (if any) in the independent testing done by the evaluation lab. You are obligated to demonstrate that you have tested the security functions and recorded the results. This will include the test plans, test scripts, and expected and actual test results.

Vulnerability Assessment
- AVA_VAN.2 - Vulnerability analysis

At EAL 2, the evaluator will check public domain sources of vulnerabilities such as SecurityFocus and U.S. Computer Emergency Readiness Team (US-CERT) websites for vulnerability information that may be applicable to the TOE. You may be required to explain how the TOE is not susceptible to the vulnerabilities reported on the public websites. The evaluator will also perform penetration tests based on information provided in the design documents.

EAL 3 Requirements

EAL 3 builds on top of the requirements in EAL 2. Below are the additional requirements for EAL 3 over EAL 2.

Development
- ADV_FSP.3 - Functional specification with complete summary
- ADV_TDS.2 - Architectural design

There are just a few differences between EAL 2 and EAL 3, but there are a couple of areas that may prove to be difficult to address if you don't have sufficient existing internal documentation.

The functional specification and architecture design requirements of EAL 3 require documentation on not only the security-enforcing actions but also the security-supporting and non-interfering actions. This probably increases the amount of work in this area over EAL 2 considerably if there is no existing design documentation to draw upon.

Lifecycle Support
- ALC_CMC.3 - Authorization controls
- ALC_CMS.3 - Implementation representation and CM coverage
- ALC_DVS.1 – Identification of security measures
- ALC_LCD.1 – Developer-defined lifecycle model

There are minor differences in the configuration management requirements at EAL 3 over EAL 2, but the addition of development security and lifecycle maintenance requirements may require some significant work if you haven't already established a development security program or a standard secure product development lifecycle.

Tests
- ATE_COV.2 - Analysis of coverage
- ATE_DPT.1 - Testing: basic design

EAL 3 requires a bit more documentation to illustrate the connection between the tests and the functional specifications. EAL 3 also adds an analysis of the depth of testing. These are relatively minor incremental documentation efforts.

EAL 4 Requirements

EAL 4 is the highest assurance level that is internationally recognized. There are significant differences between amount of effort required to prepare for and meet EAL 4 requirements over EAL 3 or 2. Below are the additional requirements for EAL 4 over EAL 3.

Development
- ADV_FSP.4 - Complete functional specification
- ADV_IMP.1 - Implementation representation of the TSF
- ADV_TDS.3 - Basic modular design

EAL 4 development evidence documents must describe the TOE to the module-level (i.e. breakdown of subsystems), all of the parameters, actions and error messages. This requires a much more in-depth description of the TOE and all of its component parts. This is analogous to the difference between high-level design and low-level design documentation.

Lifecycle Support
- ALC_CMC.4 - Production support, acceptance procedures and automation
- ALC_CMS.4 - Problem tracking CM coverage
- ALC_TAT.1 - Well-defined development tools

The biggest differentiator for EAL 4 is the requirement to provide the *implementation representation* or source code for the TOE. The evaluator will use this to verify design documentation and develop more in-depth tests and vulnerability analysis. Some vendors are concerned about releasing source code to third-parties, so this may be a topic to discuss with your business executives and legal personnel.

The configuration management system must support automation (i.e. automated builds) for the TOE as well as problem/defect tracking. Those vendors that use manual processes to build their products may not meet the EAL 4 requirements. Defect tracking systems are not always integrated with configuration management, so some system modifications may be required to meet these requirements.

Vulnerability Assessment
- AVA_VAN.3 - Focused vulnerability analysis

The evaluator performs penetration testing using the evidence documentation provided by the vendor. There is no additional effort required by the vendor however.

Avoid Misuing CC Evaluations

I'd like to point a few things that the CC is not. I raise these points because I've been involved in lengthy, and sometimes heated, discussions (primarily with product managers) about these things that only add time, cost and risk to the evaluation project but yield little or no benefit. In terms of managing project scope, here are some things to avoid.

I have found that the CC is not a good way to market competitive features. Product managers (PM) sometimes think of CC evaluations as if they were one of those magazine product test reports such as in *PC Magazine*. The PM would like to advertise the fact that his/her product has a unique way of displaying data or has faster throughput. They think that if they could somehow include that feature as part of the CC evaluation, customers would recognize it and want to buy the product. This doesn't work for a couple of reasons. First, the only place the product security features are publicly shown in CC evaluations is in the ST which is written in CC language and thus only understandable by CC geeks. Second, unless the feature is a CC-relevant security feature, it is not appropriate in a CC evaluation.

CC evaluations are also not a quick and easy way to test product features. I had one PM try to use the test phase of the CC evaluation as a way to test other product features that were not part of the evaluation. I guess his purpose was to be able to advertise that an independent third-party had done some product testing on a feature where the competition had not. Any extraneous work wastes time and increases the risk that the CC evaluation might not be completed on schedule. I'll discuss more about controlling project scope later in this book.

CC is not a replacement for the more well-known Federal Information Processing Standard 140 (FIPS 140) cryptographic module validation and vice versa. The FIPS 140 cryptographic module validation program (CMVP) [CMVP] is managed by the U.S. National Institute of Standards and Technology (NIST) and the Canadian Communications Security Establishment (CSE) to evaluate the security and quality of only cryptographic modules. According to the CMVP website [CMVP], a Common Criteria evaluation does not replace a FIPS 140 cryptographic module validation. There is no mapping or comparison between the CC EALs and the FIPS 140 levels. A CC certificate will not be a substitute for a FIPS 140 certificate or vice-versa.

Finally, CC evaluations are not a good indicator of how well the certified product secures a customer's environment. Evaluations do not guarantee security. Evaluations only indicate that for the evaluated configuration in the evaluation test environment, the product met the stated security requirements. Just as the EAL does not give you a security score, the CC evaluation gives no information about how secure the product will be in any particular customer's environment.

Minimize Changes to the Plan

In addition to minimizing the initial project scope, it is equally important to minimize changes to the plan during the project. Like any project, changes are almost inevitable, but minimizing the changes and the impact of those changes is the key to ensuring successful completion.

During many of the product development projects I've led, customer opportunities arose - opportunities to increase our business with them if we can deliver some additional features to them quickly. I recall one instance when we were well into an EAL 2 evaluation and a sales representative called and told me he had a customer offering a sizable contract for the product to be evaluated at EAL 4. In that case, after analyzing the potential benefits against the potential risks, we chose to complete the EAL 2 evaluation and forgo the EAL 4 opportunity. Again, my concern was that we might not complete the EAL 4 evaluation and would have nothing to show for our efforts.

A negative impact of poor resource allocation and inadequate planning is that development or QA personnel may get pulled off the CC evaluation effort to work on some other project. Of course, the other project may be something as important as a customer escalation or a high-priority product release, but these still represent a risk to successfully completing the CC evaluation. Having an executive sponsor or champion can help to minimize the resource impact if developers need to be pulled off your evaluation project.

You should carefully analyze and resist, if possible, changes to the evaluation plan such as:

- Adding platforms to the evaluation
- Changing system configurations
- Changing product versions
- Adding evaluated product features

As with many projects, there will be delays during CC evaluations. Estimates for gathering information or producing documents may have been too optimistic, or unforeseen circumstances interfered with the planned completion of certain milestones. In past CC evaluations, I've coordinated with our evaluation lab to work around delayed deliverables. For example, *configuration management* (CM) documentation is oftentimes the first evidence evaluated by the lab, but in one project because it took longer than expected to gather the details about the source code management system tool the development team used, the CM document completion was delayed. I worked with our CC evaluation lab to have them begin to review the user guidance instead of the CM documentation until the CM documentation was completed and ready for evaluation. This resulted in a slip of the CM evaluation work, but moved up the guidance evaluation completion date. The net result was a minimal impact on the overall schedule. You should always look for opportunities to maintain the overall project schedule even if the internal milestones have to shift.

I (and other vendors) have encountered situations where unanticipated issues arose which required a significant change in not only the evaluation plans but the product release plans as well. In one case, the evaluator advised the vendor (late in the evaluation process) that the TOE should log the audit logging mechanism's start and stop events – that is, when auditing was turned on or off should be logged to prevent tampering. The product did not support this functionality and a patch had to be produced to add this feature; this resulted in a disruption of development schedules and some evaluation rework.

Leverage Evidence

A valuable exercise that I conduct with the product development team before we begin a CC evaluation project is a pre-evaluation assessment. This exercise assesses our preparedness for the evaluation and helps identify opportunities to minimize time risk. This requires that we do our homework to understand the customer requirements and have some understanding for the product. I have developed a questionnaire which asks detailed questions about the product features based on potential *security functional requirements* (SFR) that can be claimed in the *Security Target* (ST). I also have a set of questions about the product development process and the existence of certain internal documents such as user guides for the source code configuration management system, the product delivery processes, and secure product configuration guidance.

With this information, we can determine what information is missing or not documented. This will highlight what holes need to be filled in terms of evaluation evidence. The more holes you have to fill, the more time and money you have to spend. If CC documentation already existed or was developed as a "normal" part of the product development process, then some time can be saved. Companies such as Oracle Corporation [Oracle] build these deliverables into their development processes and thus are well-prepared for evaluations.

Here are some "typical" internal documents that can either be submitted directly as CC evidence or contain the critical information for CC evaluations:

- Product marketing literature containing descriptions of features
- Product architecture block diagram
- Internal design documents
- Source code (although you really don't want to have to look at source code if you don't have to)
- Test plans (and test scripts)
- Delivery processes
- Source code control system tool documentation
- System engineering training materials

The value of these documents for CC evaluations comes from the security-relevant content (as defined by the CC) they contain. That is, internal documents that describe functions but don't describe how those functions operate securely are of little value to CC evaluators. Also, documents that don't reflect current reality are of little use. Too often, engineering documents haven't been kept up-to-date; this makes the security evaluators and government officials incredulous. This is one reason why they don't trust commercial products and why they developed things like CC evaluations.

After completing several CC evaluations, I found that we were able to reuse some evidence from previous evaluations. Because the product teams used some of the same tools and follow the same corporate standard processes, we were able to reuse evidence documentation from previous CC evaluations. Some of the documents we reused were:

- Delivery process documents since all products used the same manufacturing and distribution mechanisms
- Configuration management source code control system tool user instructions

I found that going through many CC evaluations highlights the advantage of standardizing processes across the company and documenting them. This reuse saved us tens of thousands of dollars in evidence development costs for each evaluation and saved us dozens of person-hours in time.

CC-Specific Documentation

Some CC evaluation labs would claim that there is no need to generate CC-specific evidence documents. They would also claim vendors can save money by not hiring a CC consultant to write the evidence documentation. Perhaps they believe that internal product documentation have sufficient information about product security. I have not found that to be true in practice. I was involved in one CC evaluation where we felt the internal design documentation would sufficiently cover the requirements of the CC evaluator. We handed over all of the design documents related to the TOE functionality along with design documents for modules adjacent to the TOE. The CC evaluators trudged through the documents trying to extract the CC security-relevant information they needed to satisfy their requirements. After many weeks of effort dredging up additional documents and responding to evaluation reports, we gave up. We certainly did not make it easy for the evaluator to do their job and we paid for it.

Chapter 8: Partner Selection

An extremely important set of decisions you have to make early on is the selection of partners you will employ during the CC evaluation process. The competence and experience of these parties along with the quality of the relationship you establish with them will dictate how successful your evaluation project will be. These partners include:

1. Scheme
2. Evaluation lab
3. CC Consultant

Selection Criteria

In selecting partners in CC evaluation projects, due diligence is an absolute must. I've identified 4 key factors that should be included in your due diligence process for selecting CC evaluation partners. Each factor is more or less important depending on what role the partner plays in the CC evaluation. The key factors are:

- Technical Expertise
- Total Costs
- Contract Terms
- Cooperative Relationship

Technical Expertise

The partners you hire are expected to be experts in the Common Criteria. They need to have demonstrated that they have successfully completed several CC evaluations. The Schemes, by definition, are the national authorities of the Common Criteria. However, there is a great deal of variance in expertise and experience among CC evaluation labs and CC consultants. By checking the Common Criteria Portal or the national Scheme websites, you can see which CC evaluation labs have performed the most CC evaluations. The Recent Evaluations table at the end of this book contains information about the products, vendors, Schemes and evaluation labs involved in CC evaluations completed by April 2010. Uncovering which CC consultants have the most experience is much more challenging because that information is not generally publicly available.

Technical expertise applies not only to experience with CC evaluations but also to experience and technical knowledge about your product's technology. You can check the Common Criteria Portal website to see which CC evaluation labs and Schemes have experience with products similar to the one you want evaluated. The more familiar your CC consultant or CC evaluation lab is with your product technology, the less time and money you have to spend to bring them up-to-speed. It is critical to the success of the evaluation that your partners understand how your product technology works.

An associate of mine had an application software product that ran on the Novell operating system. In the middle of the CC evaluation of that product, an evaluator asked if Novell ran on Windows or UNIX - apparently not understanding that there are more than 2 operating systems in the world. Such experiences can cause serious delays in the project.

I have found that it is important to not only learn about the partner company's collective experience but it is equally important to learn about the individuals who may be working on your project. CC consultants and CC evaluation labs will share with you the resumes of their employees if you ask for them. You should be looking for people who have the kind of background that matches the type of product you want evaluated. You should also look at the depth of the team because employee turnover is a business reality. If replacements are made in the middle of the project, you want some assurance that there are others who are equally adept and knowledgeable.

Consider that the CC consultant will need to clearly and accurately describe some of the intimate details of your product's operation and how it operates securely. S/he will also be describing your development and delivery processes. The CC evaluation lab you select will be examining documentation and checking the content details against the CC standards. You want these people to not only know the evaluation process but be able to quickly learn the intricacies of your product.

In my experience, some of the product development and QA team members involved in CC evaluations have had to spend an inordinate amount of time teaching CC evaluation labs how to install, configure and operate their products. In a couple of instances, we sent the CC evaluators to customer and systems engineering classes held at our sales offices so they could learn how to use the products. These efforts cost money and take time. Minimally, you should strive to find partners who already have some background knowledge about your product technology and have demonstrated the ability to learn quickly.

Total Costs

In the previous chapter, I discussed the need to manage the project scope to constrain and control the costs. As with any due diligence exercise, you should get as many competitive quotes or estimates from your prospective partners as possible. When obtaining initial estimates, be sure all of the various costs are included such as travel costs and other expenses. It is important to understand the partners' overhead rates. Overhead costs pay for things for which you may not gain any direct benefit (e.g. desks in the evaluation lab or the employee exercise room). Obviously, seek partners with lower overhead rates.

Price comparison is very difficult for CC evaluation labs and CC consultants. There is very little public data available and what data is available takes time to collect. You will generally need to request cost estimates and quotes directly from each party individually. My experience has been that trying to compare estimates from different companies is truly an "apples-to-oranges" comparison. No two companies will provide cost information in a comparable way. Price comparison with other product vendors with similar products is of little help because the product you build and the processes you use will be different from any other product vendor. Be prepared to do some analysis once you get the cost data from the providers.

Some partners will deliver quotes while others will give you estimates. Read the quotes and estimates carefully and note that estimates are hardly worth the paper they are written on and are subject to cost overruns. Also, many of the contracts I've negotiated with vendors included a clause that said I could not share the detailed figures with anyone, so I share only approximations or aggregations of prices in this book.

Contract Terms

The big question with contract terms is do you go for fixed price or *time and materials* (T&M)? Both types have advantages and disadvantages. Both require that you do some homework up-front. There seem to be a limited number of CC evaluation labs and CC consultants that offer fixed price contract terms. This seems natural since the CC evaluation process is non-deterministic. Evidence rework and delays can occur by no fault of the consultant or the evaluation lab. Evaluation rework means someone has to modify the evidence, re-submit it, and the evaluator has to spend more time re-evaluating the modified document. This takes time and costs money. If the rework is required because the product vendor failed to explain something fully or accurately, shouldn't the cost for rework be paid by the vendor? However, if the CC consultant or CC evaluation lab are at fault due to incompetence or error, they should bear the additional cost. From the product vendor's point of view, you want to control costs, reduce risk and incentivize behavior to your advantage.

In CC evaluations, one of the key reasons why the projects run over budget and over time is that evidence has to be reworked excessively. For example, during one evaluation, we submitted a functional specification document to the evaluation lab. The evaluators reviewed the document and found some naming and labeling discrepancies between the functional specifications and the Security Target. The functional specification document was updated, re-submitted and re-evaluated. Because we had a *time and materials* contract, this required additional cost to cover the rework effort. Fixed-price contracts would have prevented us from having to pay extra for the rework effort. Fixed-price contracts make budgeting more predictable and also incentivize the service provider to minimize rework; this pushes the provider to do a good job the first time through. However, fixed-price contracts costs are developed assuming some amount of rework will be involved, so you may end up paying a premium for a fixed-price contract.

Description	Rate	Hours	Total
Estimated ideal case hours	$150	700	$105,000
Estimated rework hours	$150	200	$30,000
Overhead costs			$15,000
Total fixed-price bid			**$150,000**

Table 14: Example Fixed Price Scenario

In the example shown in Table 14, if there was no rework, the cost would be $105,000 plus the $15,000 overhead costs or $120,000. This is basically equivalent to a T&M contract where everything went smoothly. The fixed-price bidder will almost always account for some amount of rework or unexpected costs and build that into the contracted bid. In this example, the additional $30,000 is added to cover these cases. Experienced and successful CC evaluation labs and consultants are able to accurately estimate the amount of rework so that they don't lose money during the project. Inexperienced ones may either offer bids too low (and perhaps charging you extra later) or too high (and making you pay a high premium).

Some vendors will provide "fixed price plus" contract terms. These contracts have provisions to add time and material costs when the fixed price assumptions have been exceeded. For example, I worked with an evaluation lab that reworked some development evidence through 2 revisions. Half way through the evaluation of the third revision, I was notified that we would have to pay them on an hourly rate to continue through that work unit. The contract was not clear about when this hourly rate condition would occur, but it was clear that the evaluation lab's fixed price assumption was that they would spend no more than two and a half evaluations on any single work unit. Be sure you understand under what conditions your fixed price contract remains in force.

Time and material contracts usually make it quite clear what you are paying for. These contracts have all of the itemized details – hourly rate of the evaluator, overhead, travel and other expenses. If you receive a T&M bid from someone that doesn't have that level of detail, ask for the details; you will need it. T&M contracts will generally have an estimate for the number of person-hours it will take to complete the project. Again, most T&M contracts will tell you how much time they estimate they will spend on each phase or work unit. The person-hours are only estimates and if rework is required, you will pay for the additional hours of effort at the contracted rate.

Description	Rate	Hours	Total
Estimated ideal case hours	$150	700	$105,000
Overhead costs			$15,000
Estimated T&M costs			**$120,000**

Table 15: Time and Materials Example

In the T&M example shown in Table 15, the estimated costs are lower than the previous fixed-price bid because this is only an estimate.

I worked closely with our corporate purchasing department on many of the contracts I negotiated with CC evaluation labs and consultants. I've found the purchasing department to be helpful in defining and following company-standard due diligence practices. They helped create the statement of work or request for quote and included our company standard contracting terms (for insurance, etc.) They also were good at making sure that I put a cap or maximum amount on the purchase order that would be reflected in my budget. Most contracts that I've created included a not-to-exceed amount because that represented a budget limit that would require a vice president's approval to allocate additional funding for the project. The maximum amount I usually include in the T&M contract is similar to the fixed-price contract example.

Table 16 summarizes the advantages and disadvantages of the different contract types.

Option	Advantage	Disadvantage
Fixed-price	Predictable costs	Premium price
Time and Materials	Lower cost potential	Rework drives costs up

Table 16: Fixed Price vs. T&M

Cooperative Relationship

Besides the hard, analytical analysis of partner selection, I think it is important to consider some "touchy-feely" aspects of this analysis. I have found that the cooperative, collaborative relationships I have developed with my partners in the CC evaluation projects have contributed greatly to the success of these projects. I have also found that adversarial relationships have led to project delays and the associated cost overruns. I also feel that the success or failure of the evaluation project will be determined by the relationship between your CC consultant and your evaluation lab and the relationship between the lab and the Scheme.

In one CC evaluation our CC consultant, who was new to the CC process, argued with the evaluator over the interpretation of a SFR in the intrusion detection system Protection Profile. The consultant spent days going back-and-forth with the evaluator – writing emails, making phone calls and spending time researching new arguments. Meanwhile, we were paying both parties to argue with each other. This led to both of them thinking the other was incompetent and belligerent. The relationship never improved and we ended up changing consultants. In contrast, the last several CC evaluations I was involved in went quite smoothly because the consultant and evaluation lab had mutual respect for one another.

As with any personal relationship, it may take time to develop and assess your relationships with your CC consultant and evaluation lab. The sooner you can do that assessment and establish a cooperative relationship, the better. Technical competence is always a good way to start to gain the respect of others, but equally important is the ability to listen and hear the concerns and constraints of the other parties and to be flexible to accommodate them. They will in turn be more likely to be flexible with you.

As with any due diligence process, you should check references. Ask the provider for as many references as they have. You should be sure to check with references that have completed CC evaluations similar to yours. Of course, you probably won't get much (if any) information from direct competitors, but it probably won't hurt to ask. When I mean "similar evaluations", I mean similar EAL levels, similar product types, and similar platforms. You should ask the reference open ended questions about the general experience they had with the service provider. You should also ask more detailed questions about the length of time it took and what issues or problems they encountered and how they resolved them.

Beyond the set of references the CC evaluation lab or consultant provides, you may also want to check informally with other product vendors to find out which providers they use and which ones they like and why. The Common Criteria Vendors' Forum [CCVF] was established to help vendors share this type of information and to establish connections between vendors. The annual International Common Criteria Conference is the other place to meet other product vendors, CC evaluation labs, and consultants face-to-face. This conference will give you exposure to the international scene and to a great many experts in the field.

Factor Summary

Table 17 summarizes the importance of the different factors discussed in this section relative to the different service providers.

Provider	Technical	Costs	Contract Terms	Relationship
Scheme	High importance	Not much choice	No choice	Important
Evaluation Lab	High importance	Shop around	Shop around	High importance
Consultant	High importance	Shop around	Shop around	High importance

Table 17: Partner Selection Summary

Schemes

Because of international mutual recognition of CC evaluations, vendors can take their products to any one of the certificate-authorizing nations to have products evaluated. At the time of this writing, the set of CC *certificate-authorizing* countries are listed in Table 18. The current list of *certificate-authorizing* countries can be found on the Common Criteria Portal website [CC Portal].

Each of these countries has a CC Scheme that governs that countries implementation of the Common Criteria and is responsible for issuing the actual certificates. Implementation of the CC in each nation means the Scheme is responsible for establishing polices around the use of the CC standards and to establish and maintain national interpretations of the standards. As with all international standards, there is always room for interpretation and each Scheme is afforded the flexibility to interpret the standards and augment them so that each nation satisfies their information security and privacy requirements. As such, there is some variability in the way CC evaluations and validations are conducted across the globe. These variations can be an advantage or a hindrance to the vendor attempting to complete their CC evaluation. You should understand what those differences are and how they might affect your evaluation.

• Australia	• New Zealand
• Canada	• France
• Germany	• Italy
• Japan	• Republic of (South) Korea
• The Netherlands	• Norway
• Spain	• Sweden
• United Kingdom	• United States of America

Table 18: Certificate-Authorizing Countries

In my years managing CC evaluations, I had products evaluated in the U.K., U.S. and Canada. I have seen some marked differences in the way each Scheme approaches the Common Criteria. I have heard some complaints from some nations that other nations' Schemes were not rigorous enough. If you want to just minimize the cost of CC evaluations, you want to seek out those Schemes that have a reputation for being "lenient." From my experience, I have noted that different Schemes seem to focus their attention on different things such as consistency in the use of terms in the CC evidence documentation or emphasizing product testing. I would say that not only are there differences between Schemes, but there are differences in individual validators (certifiers) within Schemes. One of the complaints about the Common Criteria is the lack of consistency across Schemes since many have national interpretations and there are differences in validators and evaluators.

atsec, a CC evaluation lab that has been accredited to conduct evaluations in the U.S., Germany and Sweden produced a report called "Common Criteria: National Validation Scheme Differences: CCEVS, CSEC and BSI" [atsec]. CCEVS is the Common Criteria Evaluation and Validations Scheme [CCEVS] in the U.S. CSEC is the Swedish Sveriges Certifieringsorgan, the Swedish CC Scheme. BSI is the Bundemsamt fur Sicherheit in der Informationstechnik, the German CC Scheme [BSI]. This report provides some information about the following considerations for each of the three Schemes:

- Validation costs
- Scheme travel expenses
- Tax
- Product restrictions
- Prerequisites for evaluation
- Project progress
- Initial kickoff meeting
- Validation oversight
- CC interpretations
- Cryptographic policies
- Site visits
- Certification phase and issuance of certificate

Sweden and Germany charge a validation fee. Although the U.S. considered charging a validation fee a few years ago, that program never progressed. Similarly, Sweden and Germany charge a fee for travel required for site visits. Applicable value added taxes (VAT) are applied to validation services.

To my knowledge, all of the Schemes prioritize acceptance of products based on their national use. That is, if a product is used within that country, it will be given preference for acceptance into validation over products that are not used in that country, particularly by that country's government.

One of the key prerequisites for all of these Schemes is that a draft Security Target must be submitted before a product will be accepted into validation. They also require an evaluation plan or schedule outlining the timetable for the project as a prerequisite.

Germany and the U.S. have policies and procedures for aborting validation efforts if there is an apparent lack of progress; however, all three Schemes have some form of on-going validation oversight to monitor the progress of the evaluation.

All have national interpretations that are posted on the Scheme websites. Germany has no cryptographic policy while the U.S. and Sweden do in accordance with their national regulations. German validators are required to attend the vendor site visit. Swedish validators shall be invited but may attend at their discretion. U.S. validators do not normally participate in site visits. Each Scheme has different time schedules for when the certificate will be available after the evaluation phase has completed.

CC Evaluation Labs

Each national Scheme oversees the evaluation work of a number of evaluation labs accredited to conduct CC evaluations in that country. Here is the list of accredited CC evaluations testing labs (CCTL) around the world as of May 2010:

Australia and New Zealand
- CSC
- Logica
- stratsec

Canada
- CGI Information Systems and Management Consultants Inc.
- DOMUS IT Security Laboratory
- EWA – Canada

France
- CESTI-AQL - Groupe SILICOMP-AQL
- CEA - LETI
- CEACI (THALES - CNES)
- Oppida
- Serma Technologies - ITSEF

Germany

- Atos Origin GmbH
- atsec information security GmbH
- brightsight bv
- CSC Deutschland Solutions GmbH
- datenschutz nord GmbH
- Deutsches Forschungszentrum für künstliche Intelligenz GmbH
- media transfer AG
- secunet SwissIT AG
- SRC Security Research & Consulting GmbH
- Tele-Consulting
- T-Systems GEI GmbH
- TÜV Informationstechnik GmbH

Italy

- Consorzio RES
- IMQ/LPS
- Proge-Sec
- LVS - Eutelia S.p.A.
- Technis Blu Srl
- GFI Security Lab

Japan

- Information Technology Security Center Evaluation Department
- Electronic Commerce Security Technology Laboratory Inc.
- Mizuho Information & Research Institute, Inc.
- TÜV Informationstechnik GmbH

The Republic of Korea

- KISA - IT Security Evaluation Center
- Korea Testing Laboratory (KTL)
- Korea System Assurance (KOSYAS)
- Korea Security Evaluation Laboratory (KSEL)
- Telecommunications Technology Association (TTA)

The Netherlands

- Brightsight bv

Norway
- Aspect Labs
- brightsight bv
- Norconsult ITSEF
- Secode Norge AS

Spain
- Centro de Evaluación de la Seguridad de las Tecnologías de la Información (CESTI)
- Applus
- Epoche and Espri

Sweden
- atsec information security AB
- Combitech AB

United Kingdom
- EDS
- Logica
- SiVenture

United States
- Arca
- atsec information security corporation
- Booz Allen Hamilton
- COACT Inc.
- Computer Sciences Corporation
- CygnaCom Solutions
- DSD Information Assurance Laboratory (DIAL)
- InfoGard Laboratories, Inc
- SAIC

     I have experience dealing with several U.S. labs, a U.K. lab, and a Canadian lab for the variety of CC evaluations conducted over the years. We started with a U.K. lab primarily because European customers were demanding CC evaluations of our gateway firewall and the U.K. had the most experience testing firewalls. We tried a couple of U.S. labs because the currency exchange rate with the U.K. made continuing with them cost-prohibitive. We ran into issues with the U.S. labs and tried a

Canadian lab. We considered several factors in selecting the CC evaluations labs. These factors included:

- Technical competence and experience
- Costs and advantageous contract terms
- Spoken and written language and time zone issues

Technical Competence and Experience

Since vendors are paying the CC evaluation lab personnel to come up to speed on the product technology, it is beneficial to work with a lab that has experience with similar technologies. For example, we chose a U.K. lab to evaluate our gateway firewall because they had experience evaluating firewalls. We didn't have to spend much time with them explaining how our product worked.

Some vendors have expressed concern that CC evaluation labs gain access to some proprietary information and could leak that information (maliciously or inadvertently) to competitors who bring their products to that lab. For the chronically paranoid, I will acknowledge there is a possibility of some leakage occurring; however, the reputation and viability in this business relies heavily upon the lab to maintain strict confidentiality of such information.

Switching Costs

You will invest considerable time helping your evaluation lab understand your product technologies, your development processes, and your evidence documentation. Should you consider switching evaluation labs either in the middle of an evaluation or for a subsequent one for the same product, be aware that the switching costs can be considerable. Conversely, there is an advantage to using the same lab for subsequent evaluations of the same product – in particular assurance maintenance. This can make negotiating renewal contracts with evaluation labs a bit more difficult because you lose some leverage.

Contracts and Advantageous Contract Terms

Contracts with CC evaluation labs can be tricky. You have to decide whether you should consider fixed-price contracts or time and materials contracts or some combination. Fixed price contracts generally are formulated with some conservative (from the evaluation lab's perspective) cost figures so in the ideal situation, you could end up paying more with a fixed-price contract than with a time and materials contract. The time and materials contract allows you to pay for only the time it takes to get the job done.

I have experience with a variety of contract options including a fixed price contract with a portion (site visit and some rework) covered by a time and material provision. I preferred the fixed price contract (with a trusted, competent lab – of course) over the time and material contact because the fixed price contract promotes the most advantageous behavior from the CC evaluation lab and it is easier to budget over multiple fiscal quarters.

As I will explain later, the CC evaluation process is a series of cycles through producing evidence, evaluating evidence, producing comments, revising evidence and re-evaluating the revisions. We go through these cycles until the evaluator is satisfied that the evidence provides complete and accurate information in accordance with the CC standards. Under a time and materials contract, the more cycles you have to go through, the more it costs. I have been in situations where the evaluator decided to nit-pick some details and kept sending evidence back to us for revisions and further re-evaluation. This resulted in some expensive loops.

Fixed price contracts tend to eliminate the temptation for the evaluator to nit-pick and send evidence back for rework. Fixed price contracts are generally priced such that it assumes a reasonable number of rework cycles (probably 2 or 2.5) so there is little incentive for the evaluation lab to propagate the rework cycles. Fixed price contracts share the risk between the CC evaluation lab and the vendor.

Spoken and Written Language and Time Zones Issues

In light of the fact that there are a number of labs in (remote) countries where the labor costs can be significantly lower you should consider any associated communication issues. You will be exchanging extensive written technical documentation and verbally discussing evaluation issues directly with the CC evaluation lab personnel. Clear and accurate communications is critical to the success of any CC evaluation.

While time zone differences may appear to be a minor inconvenience with today's technologies, you may find that there will be inherent delays in responding to requests thus slowing the overall progress of the evaluation project.

Do not underestimate the importance of being able to communicate clearly with your evaluation lab partners. If their native language is not your native language, you will encounter misunderstandings during the exchange of evidence documentation and evaluation verdicts. CC evaluations have its own language, but communicating the nuances, interpretations and assumptions can be tricky especially if you and the evaluator do not speak and write in the same natural language.

Even if a foreign lab offers a lower cost bid, you should take into account the real possibilities of delays due to miscommunications and time zone delays.

CC Consultants

CC consultants offer a variety of services to product vendors to help them meet the requirements of CC evaluations. CC consultants can provide training to development staff members to acquaint them with the evaluation process. They can also do the writing necessary to produce the evidence documentation to be delivered to the evaluators. Some even provide project management services.

Buy Versus Build

The very first thing you need to decide when considering CC consultants is whether to do the CC evidence development with in-house resources or outsource the effort to a third-party. This "buy versus build" analysis of evidence development will have a significant impact on your pre-evacuation planning. My experience has shown that you can spend almost an equal amount in third-party consulting as in CC evaluation lab costs, so CC consultants can eat up a significant portion of your budget.

Many vendors I know do not use CC consultants. They do their own in-house evidence development, project management and training. Most of these vendors are experienced. Obviously, the advantage of not using a CC consultant is that you don't have to pay someone else and their overhead. The disadvantage is that if you don't know what you are doing, you can waste a lot of time and effort. As a novice, should you decide to "go it alone" without the aid of a CC consultant – beware. There are a myriad of nuances and interpretations of the CC standards that can't be discovered by reading the ISO/CC standards alone. For example, when a security requirement states "the TOE shall protect user data", what does that mean exactly to the CC evaluator and what does it take to prove it?

Table 19 summarizes the advantages and disadvantages of in-house and outsourced evidence development options.

Option	Advantages	Disadvantages
In-house	Reduced expenses	Not a core competency Lost opportunities
Outsource	Use CC expertise	Risk of incompetence Increased expenses

Table 19: In-house vs. Outsource

Good and Bad Consultants

Theoretically, CC consultants are the experts and should help novice vendors navigate efficiently through the evaluation process. In reality, there are good CC consultants and there are bad CC consultants. A good consultant knows how to smoothly and efficiently get through the evaluation process with little fuss and delay. A bad consultant can lead you to an aborted evaluation attempt after taking a bunch of your money with him/her. How can you tell the difference? You can either use trial-and-error (as I did) until you find someone who is competent or you can leverage the knowledge and experience of others. One of the reasons the Common Criteria Vendors' Forum [CCVF] was created was to share information about the process and to share experiences. While some members work for competing companies, there are many others who are not competitors and are willing to share their experiences.

The last several CC evaluations I led used the same consultant; this was someone who understood the vendor's perspective having worked for a product company himself in the past. He also was very experienced in CC evaluations having led many product evaluation efforts with his former company. This vendor perspective was a critical factor in my decision to use his services. Other consultants I tried did not understand the limitations and pressures on the product vendors.

These other consultants seemed to understand the theory of CC but did not appreciate the product development realities of its implementation.

The good CC consultant will offer the product development team a brief training session on the CC evaluation process. The good CC consultant will focus on the aspects of the CC that directly affect the roles and responsibilities of the developers. I've had consultants waste my time by giving me a lecture on the history of the CC. I've also had a CC consultant review the CC standards one requirement at a time even if they were not relevant to the target product. A good CC consultant will do his/her homework first by reviewing product user documentation to understand its functionality. S/he can then tailor the CC training to focus on what is relevant to the product. The CC consultant should also describe the overall process and set expectations appropriately so that the development team is well-prepared to engage fully.

Since I was directly involved in so many CC evaluations and I have a development background, I conducted customized CC training sessions for many development teams myself. Since I also was familiar with many of the existing internal processes, I could also conduct the pre-evaluation assessments and gap analyses in preparation for the evaluations.

I used CC consultants primarily as technical writers to produce the evidence documentation to be delivered to the CC evaluation lab. While some CC evaluation labs insist it is not necessary for product vendors to produce CC-specific documentation to submit for evidence, I believe that approach is insufficient and inefficient. Based on my experience and observation, I would say that most product vendors do not have the necessary evidence documentation on hand to support most CC evaluations. Although vendors should have complete and up-to-date documentation on the product design and development procedures, many do not. Audrey Dale, former NIAP director, remarked to me once that she was surprised by the lack of security documentation vendors normally have available. Also, even if vendors have documentation that describe product designs or process descriptions, CC evaluators may find it difficult and time-consuming to sort out the information they need to meet the CEM requirements. In one evaluation, we tried handing over volumes of design documentation to the CC evaluation lab as evidence, but the evaluators ended up spending so much time trying to extract the CC relevant information that we had to scrap that idea. Given that we were paying the evaluators on a time-and-materials basis at the time, it cost us a small fortune.

The key advantage of using a good, experienced CC consultant to develop the evidence documentation is that s/he knows what the CC evaluator is looking for. S/he also knows how to make sure the variety of documents are self-consistent. We had experiences where in-house developed documents submitted to the CC evaluation lab were rejected because terminology was not used consistently (e.g. we called a module "Admin Console" in one document and "Manager" in another). Confusing the evaluator leads to delays and increases costs. The good CC consultant also knows how much detail is required to satisfy the evaluator and the CEM requirements. I have found that sometimes too much detail can lead to problems as well. Too much detail can lead to more questions from the evaluator as it may reveal potential vulnerabilities or inconsistencies.

Internal Technical Writers

In a few early CC evaluations I tried using internal product information development or InfoDev (technical writers) to develop the CC evidence. We abandoned that approach as the InfoDev personnel found the work unsatisfying and too different from what they were accustomed. They also felt having this unique skill set did not improve their personal marketability. We did not want to develop CC evidence creation into a core competency, so we opted to use outside consultants instead.

Evaluation Lab Consultants

Many of the companies that provide CC evaluation lab testing services also provide CC consultancy services. Several product vendors I know use them and I had at one point used them as well. An advantage of using a consultant from the same company as the CC evaluation lab is that the consultant understands the CC evaluation process partly because they probably serve as an evaluator on someone else's product. Another advantage is that there is little time delay between when the evaluator finds an issue or has a question and the time the consultant hears about it.

The disadvantage I see with using consultants from CC evaluation labs is that these consultants generally don't have an understanding for the vendor's perspective. They understand what the evaluator is looking for (which is good when writing the evidence documents), but not so good when you are trying to be expedient and cost-conscious.

Some vendors are concerned about the possible conflict of interest - having the same company produce the evidence and evaluate it. These companies provide assurances to not only the product vendors but also to their national Schemes (that accredit them) that there is a "firewall" in place between the consultant side of the house and the evaluation lab side. I, for one, do not think there is an issue here, but if you are concerned and do not accept the contracted safeguards, then work with an independent CC consultant.

Contracts

Contracts with CC consultants can be fixed price or time and materials. Once I found the CC consultant I trusted, fixed price contracts were the norm. The same arguments about fixed price versus time and material CC evaluation lab contracts apply here.

PART 3: EVIDENCE DEVELOPMENT

In this part:

Chapter 9: Evidence Development Tips

In the previous chapter, we discussed the buy-versus-build decision you must make regarding the development of CC evidence documentation. I've shared with you my experiences and decision-making process. The following chapters discuss each of the evidence types that are required for CC evaluations at *Evaluation Assurance Levels* (EAL) 1 through 4 – the levels internationally recognized and the levels most commercial vendors pursue. Before we delve into more of the details of the *Security Target* (ST), development, lifecycle support, tests, vulnerability assessment and guidance evidence, I'd like to share some general tips that were presented at some of the recent International Common Criteria Conferences (ICCC) from other vendors, evaluators and consultants. These presentations provide some different perspectives and reflect different experiences from my own but may prove useful as you make your own decisions about CC evidence development.

Who Does What Guide

Erin Connor, CC evaluation lab director at Electronic Warfare Associates – Canada (EWA-Canada), presented a talk at the 2007 International Common Criteria Conference (ICCC) [Connor 2007] called "Developer Documentation – A Who To Guide." Erin used a play on words changing the more familiar "how-to guide" title to a "who to guide" to illustrate that his analysis is about which party (developer, consultant or evaluation lab) might be most appropriate to develop the different types of evidence documentation. He makes one disclaimer at the beginning of his presentation that the analysis does not look at the costs of internal or external resources to carry out the evidence development. Nor does it look at the production schedule requirements. In my opinion, these are critical issues and are discussed in Chapter 8: Partner Selection.

The types of evidence documents EWA analyzed were the following:

- Security Target
- Security architecture
- Functional specifications
- TOE design

- Implementation representation
- Operational user guidance
- Preparative procedures
- Configuration Management (CM) capabilities
- CM scope
- Delivery
- Development security
- Flaw remediation
- Lifecycle definition
- Tools and techniques
- Test coverage
- Test depth
- Functional tests
- Independent tests
- Vulnerability assessment

For each evidence type, EWA applied 5 factors. For each factor, EWA assigned one of 3 possible rating levels - *low*, *medium* and *high* - reflecting how well the factor applied to the given circumstances for the product developer. The 5 factors were:

1. Acceptable materials exist to serve as CC document
2. Developer would learn more about their product
3. CC knowledge is needed to develop the CC document
4. Detailed developer is input needed to develop the CC document
5. Internal resource availability

EWA concluded that the developer should create the following set of evidence:

- Operational user guidance
- Preparative procedures
- Configureation Management (CM) capabilities
- CM scope
- Delivery
- Development security
- Flaw remediation
- Lifecycle definition
- Tools and techniques
- Test coverage

- Test depth
- Functional tests

EWA determined that the following evidence should be developed jointly between the developer, evaluators and consultant:

- Security architecture
- Functional specifications
- TOE design
- Implementation representation
- Independent tests

EWA deemed that the Security Target would best be developed by the consultant and the vulnerability assessment has to be (in accordance with the CEM) developed by the evaluators.

EWA assigned a *medium* rating to the CC knowledge factor for all of the development (ADV) documents. For vendors new to CC, this is a critical factor and the *medium* rating may represent an obstacle. Design documents as well as the ST require some significant knowledge about the CC standards and the evaluation process. Some help from CC consultants or experts is definitely warranted for first-timers.

EWA gave all of the lifecycle (ALC) documents a *low* rating for CC knowledge. In my experience, while these documents may not actually require much knowledge about the CC to generate this evidence, I have found that the issue is having enough complete documentation about the development and delivery processes. Most vendors will have some documentation describing their use of configuration management or their delivery processes, but they may not be complete. Sometimes it helps to have a more objective eye look at the existing documents to point out gaps or inconsistencies in the existing documents.

From a vendor's perspective, the fifth factor – Internal Resource Availability (that EWA skipped over) may be the most important factor to consider because developers are always busy working towards their next release. What I have seen is that product developers (especially software product developers) generally hate writing, so creating documentation is not going to be easy to get them to do. Even technical writers that create customer documentation are reluctant to take on CC documentation simply because it is considered to be a specialized skill - a specialized skill that is not widely marketable.

I will also question the validity of the factor EWA called *retained intellectual property* or the notion that the developer would learn more about their product if they developed the evidence themselves. As a vendor you have to ask yourself – "do you want to know more about your product and processes and would you truly benefit from such knowledge?" You also need to know if you could be using your time more wisely. That is, what are the lost opportunity costs of doing the documentation yourself?

In most of the CC evaluation projects I led, we used a CC consultant to develop most of the evidence documentation. We did this because it saved us time. We did not have to (nor were we interested in) developing expertise in creating CC evidence documents. The next example is from a company that decided to do much more in-house evidence development.

In-House Evidence Development

Jane Medefesser, formerly with Sun Microsystems and now with Juniper Networks, presented "Vendor Strategies for Maximizing Process Under the Common Criteria" at the 2007 ICCC in Rome [Medefesser 2007]. The focus of her talk was on how to maintain schedules if you, as a vendor, decide to develop your own evidence documentation. Jane and Sun Microsystems used in-house resources to develop their CC evidence.

Jane shared her detailed schedule of the Solaris 10 release 03/05 operating system CC evaluation at EAL 4+ against the requirements in the *Controlled Access Protection Profile* (CAPP) and *Role Based Access Control Protection Profile* (RBACPP). This schedule included dates for all of the major evidence deliverables needed for the CC evaluation.

Jane's presentation went on to describe some keys to success. She discussed the need to organize and suggested that there are two organization strategies – organize by evaluation activity or organize by documentation set.

Organizing by evaluation activity broke down the documentation work into the standard evaluation work categories – Security Target, development, guidance, lifecycle, test, and vulnerability assessment. Development efforts include the creation of functional specifications, architecture and design. Test documentation includes test plans, test suites and test results.

Organization by documentation set decomposed the work into groups such as design (architecture and TOE design) and analysis (vulnerability assessment).

Since Sun and Jane's team had previously participated in several CC evaluations, there was great opportunity to reuse and recycle evidence from those previous evaluations. Flaw remediation, delivery and configuration management documents could be reused completely as the processes and tools had not changed since the previous evaluations. Misuse analysis and operational vulnerabilities documents only needed to be updated. Some other tips Jane offered were:

- Identify subject matter technical experts early and keep them available
- Be diligent about delivery of evidence to maintain the schedule
- Allow time for unexpected events that may delay the schedule

These tips confirm my own experiences and emphasize the need to adhere to strong project management practices.

Using CC Consultants

James Arnold of SAIC, a U.S.-based CC evaluation and testing laboratory, presented a talk called "Impacts of Third-Party Consultants on Common Criteria Assurances" at the 2006 ICCC in Lanzarote, Canary Islands, Spain [Arnold 2006]. James' presentation gave a unique perspective on the use of CC consultants that raised some considerations for anyone thinking about using third-party consultants for CC evidence development.

James pointed out CC consultants are used in a variety of modes - from executing simple tasks to delivering complete, turnkey solutions for evidence creation. That is, some consultants may be employed to deliver a single document or provide some guidance only. In other instances, consultants may be contracted to define, design and develop all of the CC evidence documentation for a developer. Consultants allegedly have the expertise to reduce the number of evaluation issues and reduce turnaround time thus reducing overall evaluation time. A major reason to employ CC consultants is to save time.

CC consultants can offer a spectrum of services to developers. These services range from:

- Advice
- Review
- Templates, examples or questionnaires
- Evidence creation
- Provide complete, turn-key solutions

James pointed out some important considerations when deciding on the use of consultants or how to use consultants.

- Who owns the evidence once it has been created?
- Consultants may have the same level of understanding of the CC but may have different perspectives
- Better consultants will yield better results

One of the "dangers" to think about is the potential conflict of interest if the consultant comes from the same organization as the evaluation lab. As I had pointed out earlier, most companies that offer both consulting and evaluation services ensure that there is a "firewall" between both services to avoid conflicts of interest. Of course, there is no real way to prove this, but the companies are staking their reputations and CC accreditation on their assertions.

Another consideration, no matter who develops the evidence, is that there is such a thing as providing too much information as well as too little information. By providing too much information, you may open up for examination areas that are not security relevant and just serve to distract the evaluator from the crucial parts of the evaluation. Providing too little information requires the evaluator to reject evidence and ask more questions; this just slows things down.

One of the biggest concerns for the use of third-party consultants is the learning curve the consultant has to overcome and any translation errors that might occur along the way. It takes time to learn a new technology or new product. The CC evaluators face this with every new product type they face. Similarly, the CC consultant must be able to learn what the product does and how it does it sufficiently enough to be able to document it clearly to the evaluators.

The bottom line is that developers should select consultants carefully.

BSI Guidance for Vendors

Christian Krause of the Federal Office of Information Security in Germany presented "Guideline for Developer Documentation" at the ICCC in 2007 [Krause 2007]. His presentation is based on a paper produced by BSI, the German CC Scheme, in 2007. Christian pointed out that vendors must understand the requirements within the *Common Evaluation Methodology* (CEM) in order to know what the evaluators are looking for in the CC evidence. The problem is that the CEM is written with the evaluator as the target audience, not the developer. Developers new to CC will find reading and understanding the CEM quite difficult. The CEM contains information relevant for evaluation tasks of the evaluators, not the preparation tasks of the developer. BSI recognized the difficulty developers would have in reading the CEM and then having to refer back to CC Part 3 in order to obtain the useful information they need to produce the evidence documents.

BSI developed the "Guidelines for Developer Documentation" [Developer] to serve as an aid to developers who choose to create their own CC evidence documents. This guide has extracted the pertinent developer information from the CEM and CC standards and formatted it so that is more easily understandable by developers. This guide contains explanations, examples and document templates.

The developer guide provides an overview of the assurance classes and an explanation of the differences between the EALs for the developer, evaluator and customer. It also highlights the differences from one EAL to the next higher EAL.

The guide lists all of the assurance requirements and shows for which EAL the requirement applies. It also provides the developer requirements, evaluator actions, and examples. They claim that the guide is organized such that developers can more easily find information useful to them. It is organized by assurance class just as in CC Part 3.

In my opinion, I would have found it easier to have this information organized by EAL since I would first select the EAL then I would want to know what the requirements are within that. Having to go through each class to find the requirements even with their color coding is tedious. I also found no new information for the developer that is an improvement over the descriptions in the CEM or CC Part 3. I find that this guide is still more of an aid to evaluators than to developers.

The guide also provides some templates for the evidence documents. While these templates may help developers organize the information they need to present and it may help them prevent omitting something, it looks like it would help evaluators more. If evaluators had to deal with a single, standard document format from all developers that would make their jobs easier. The standard format would be of minimal help to developers.

Automated Tools

Applus is a CC evaluation lab in Spain. They presented some information at the 2008 ICCC in South Korea [Applus 2008] about some automated tools they use to generate CC evidence documents that help reduce errors. These tools are aimed at all of the major evidence document classes – Security Target, development, guidance, lifecycle support and test. The presenters point out that some developers are reluctant to engage in CC evaluations because:

- It requires intensive CC training
- Introduces methodology changes
- Is time-consuming and expensive
- Involves too much paperwork
- Includes too much document review effort

Applus offers services to their clients that reduce or automate some of the developer effort resulting in fewer developer mistakes that might impact the successful and timely completion of the evaluation. They claim that these tools create an extensible and customizable framework and produce documentation free of errors or inconsistencies. In the ST document, their tools can identify the following types of common errors:

- Invalid references in documents
- Problems with *Security Functional Requirements* (SFR) specifications
- SFR conflicts
- Conflicts between the overview and description
- Mappings and rationale

Applus developed the tool based on Doxygen that they claim can "trace, verify and detect the lack of correctness in top-down implementation." This tool can extract subsystems and modules from the source code and check it against the developer's claims. Their tools can also generate graphics comparing the modules to the *TOE Summary Specifications*.

Individual sentences with the *Guidance* evidence can be tagged as *SFR-enforcing*, *SFR-supporting* or *SFR-non-interfering* to link them to *Development* and ST statements.

Lifecycle support evidence can be checked for confidentiality and integrity of evidence in the configuration list. This checks for the use of encryption, secure deletion and secure backup depending on the EAL.

Testing templates can be used to ensure that all of the CC test requirements are met. This also can check for consistency against the ADV evidence.

These tools and approach claim to provide benefit to evaluators and Schemes by:

- Providing a common language for coverage analysis
- Enabling traceability between evidence and assurance classes
- Integrating into CC XML structures

These tools also potentially offer the following benefits to vendors:

- Identification of problems
- Adaptable to developer tools
- Saves time and money
- Uses well-structured methodologies

French Sample Evidence

The French CC Scheme has provided an example of a set of evidence and the associated evaluation reports for a CC version 3.1 evaluation of a real product called Truecrypt [France] evaluated at EAL 2+. This material is provided as a training aid for evaluators and developers.

Truecrypt is a free, open source disk encryption software product that runs on the Microsoft Windows and Apple Mac operating systems. Its advertised features include:

- Creates a virtual encrypted disk within a file and mounts it as a real disk.
- Encrypts an entire partition or storage device such as USB flash drive or hard drive.

- Encrypts a partition or drive where Windows is installed (pre-boot authentication).
- Encryption is automatic, real-time (on-the-fly), and transparent.
- Parallelization and pipelining allow data to be read and written as fast as if the drive was not encrypted.
- Provides plausible deniability in case an adversary forces you to reveal the password
- Hidden volume (steganography) and hidden operating system.
- Encryption algorithms: AES-256, Serpent, and TwoFish. Mode of operation: XTS.

The documents provided cover the following classes consistent with the EAL 2 requirements:

- ASE – Security Target
- ADV - development
- AGD - guidance
- ALC – lifecycle support
- ATE - tests
- AVA – vulnerability assessment

I would say that this set of evidence documentation is quite thorough – the ST is 66 pages long! Certainly the uniqueness of this offering is that you can gain access to all of the detailed design and test evidence documents that you can't find elsewhere. Most vendors consider their CC evidence (other than the ST) as company-proprietary information and do not make it available to the public. As Jane Medefesser pointed out in her 2007 ICCC presentation, it is useful to be able to leverage and reuse evidence from past evaluations. Newcomers to the CC can benefit from looking at evidence from others' past evaluations just to see what format and depth is required for a real evaluation. These examples serve to provide concrete examples of what the CC and CEM attempt to describe.

Chapter 10: Security Target

Before diving into the details of the *Security Target* (ST) document, you should decide whether you ought to hire an expert CC consultant or write it yourself. As I discussed in Chapter 8: Partner Selection, you will need to do a "buy versus build" analysis to decide whether to hire third-parties or write the CC documentation yourself. This analysis should be built into your pre-evaluation planning and budgeting process.

There can be a great deal of variance in the scope and depth of each CC evaluation. This affects the amount of effort that will go into the ST. Depending on the product's complexity and how much appropriate internal documentation exists, costs will be higher or lower. In my experience, many EAL 2 evaluations of products like anti-virus, intrusion detection and e-mail security can take about 2 calendar months to conduct interviews with the technical team, read and examine internal documents, and write the ST. A less experienced person can take longer, but a CC consultant or a knowledgeable (about CC and STs) technical writer can develop the ST document in a couple of calendar-months. Most CC consultants I've employed charged $20-30K to develop a ST.

A good reference that will complement the contents of this chapter is CC Part 1 Annex A – Specification of Security Targets. This annex is basically a set of application notes that can be used as guidance in developing the ST. It provides some background and explanation for each of the sections of the ST.

Purpose of the ST

The ST is the foundation of the CC evaluation. Making mistakes in this document can have repercussions throughout the entire CC evaluation process. CC standard Part 1 defines the ST as an "implementation-specific statement of security needs for a specific identified TOE." I guess I would prefer the term "claims" in place of "needs" in the definition since the ST is a response to stated customer needs from a *Protection Profile* (PP) or other statements. The other key phrase in the definition is "specific" because the TOE being described is a specific product, not a type of product. The ST specifies the details of the *Target of Evaluation* (TOE).

Earlier in this book, I remarked that very few of the customers I've encountered actually read the ST of the evaluated product they intend to purchase, deploy and use. While this is generally the case, I think CC version 3.1 has improved the layout and readability of the ST such that customers can glean more useful information from it more easily than before. The ST is the most significant public document that is generated from the CC evaluation process. CC evaluations are intended to provide assurance to the customer that the security claims vendors make about their products are justified and the ST can serve to communicate these claims effectively.

Finally, in order for a vendor to successfully complete the first phase of their CC evaluation, that is, the *Evaluation of the ST* (ASE), I will discuss the things the evaluator will be expecting and what his/her requirements are based on the *Common Evaluation Methodology* (CEM).

ST Outline

The ST will define and bound the scope of the CC evaluation. The ST describes what will be evaluated and to what depth. The other evidence documentation that will be produced and evaluated during the course of the evaluation (e.g. functional specifications, test plans, configuration management process, etc.) will be required to be consistent with the ST. As I mentioned earlier, CC version 3.1 streamlined the format of the ST document. For example, in CC version 2.3, the *Rationale* descriptions used to be in a separate section, but with CC version 3.1, the *Rationale* is distributed across the various applicable sections. In my opinion, this makes the ST easier to read; however it seems many vendors choose to continue to keep the *Rationale* section separate. The CC version 3.1 ST outline looks like this:

1. Introduction
    o ST Reference
    o TOE Reference
    o TOE Overview
    o TOE Description
2. Conformance Claims
    o CC Version
    o PP Conformance Claims
3. Security Problem Definition
    o Threats
    o Organizational Security Policies

Introduction

The *Introduction* section of the ST contains an overview of what the product does – key features and purpose. While the product user and administrator guides provide general product feature descriptions and instructions on how to use the product, the ST highlights the security functions of the product. The objective of the ST *Introduction* evaluation activity is to determine that the ST and TOE are correctly, clearly, and consistently defined.

ST Reference

The *ST Reference* is simply the title of the Security Target document. An example is "Symantec Endpoint Security Version 12.0 Security Target." There may be a document version number or date as well to uniquely identify the document. The product name (see *TOE Reference* below) should be consistently reflected in the *ST Reference* to avoid ambiguity and confusion.

TOE Reference

The *TOE Reference* is generally the product name from which the TOE is derived. I've found that it is critical to be consistent with the naming and references throughout the ST and the rest of the CC evidence documentation. Since the CC certificate will include the identifier used in the *TOE Reference*, I've had customers verify that the product they are purchasing exactly matches the name (and version) on the certificate.

TOE Overview

The *TOE Overview* summarizes the usage and major security features of the TOE. This description can be short – generally a few paragraphs describing the TOE. This description is intended to give a brief overview of the product functions and purpose.

The *TOE Overview* also includes high-level descriptions of the security features of the product such as authentication, auditing and security management.

The *TOE Overview* will clearly identify the *TOE Type*. There doesn't seem to be a standard catalog of TOE types, but the Common Criteria Portal lists the validated products using the following categories:

- Access Control Devices and Systems
- Biometric Systems and Devices
- Boundary Protection Devices and Systems
- Data Protection
- Databases
- Detection Devices and Systems
- ICs, Smart Cards and Smart Card related Devices and Systems
- Key Management Systems
- Network and Network related Devices and Systems
- Operating systems
- Other Devices and Systems
- Products for Digital Signatures
- Trusted Computing

Finally, the *TOE Overview* will identify any non-TOE hardware, software or firmware required by the TOE. For example, Symantec Endpoint Protection (SEP) is an application software product that runs on a variety of hardware and software platforms including general purpose desktop computers supporting several flavors of Microsoft Windows operating systems. The evaluated TOE configuration for SEP included Microsoft Windows 2003, Windows XP SP 2, and Windows 2000 SP 3.

> **TOE Type Reporting**
>
> Note that when you complete your product evaluation, you will be asked to complete a form with information that will be used for the official Common Criteria Portal's validated products listing. This listing is organized by technology-type. You should carefully consider what category (TOE type) to use for your product as your customers will invariably search for your product on the Common Criteria Portal website. I paid particular attention to where competing products were listed.

TOE Description

The *TOE Description* describes the physical scope and the logical scope of the TOE. This is where a good block diagram of the system architecture and the surrounding (interfacing) IT environment comes in handy. The physical scope includes hardware, software, firmware and guidance that comprise the TOE. The logical scope gives a general description of the security functionality of the TOE.

Conformance Claims

The *Conformance Claims* section of the ST identifies conformance claims of the evaluation. The CC version (and parts) as well as any applicable protection profiles or packages are defined in this section of the ST.

CC Version

At the time of this writing (June 2010), the current version of CC is CC version 3.1. All that is required is a simple but effective statement that covers all of the necessary information required to describe the CC conformance information. Note, however, different Schemes seem to have different expectations about how this should be phrased. The CC conformance claim statement contains:

- The version of the CC used
- Either CC Part 2 conformant or CC Part 2 extended
- Either CC Part 3 conformant or CC Part 3 extended

To be Part 2 or 3 conformant means you are using only the standard security functional requirements as defined in Part 2 or security assurance requirements as defined in Part 3. If you are using Part 2 or 3 extended components, you must define your extended component definitions in this section of the ST.

This is also where the specific Evaluation Assurance Level (EAL) is reported. Any augmentation to the standard EALs will be described as well. Many vendors augment their evaluations with one of the ALC_FLR, *Flaw Remediation*, components. For example, some products will claim conformance with EAL 4 augmented with ALC_FLR.2.

PP Conformance Claims

If your ST is claiming conformance to *Protection Profile(s)* (PP), all PPs and security requirement packages to which the ST claims conformance must be listed here. Similarly, if your ST is claiming conformance to a *package,* it must list the package and describe it as either package-conformant or package-augmented. If your ST is not claiming conformance to any PP or package, this section may be eliminated.

I will not be dwelling on the concept of packages much in this book because it is infrequently used (except perhaps by the smart card community with the composition assurance package). In short, packages are a specialized set of *security functional requirements* (SFR) and/or *security assurance requirements* (SAR). *Evaluation Assurance Levels* (EAL) is a form of a package.

The evaluator will be checking for consistency between the statements in the ST against the aforementioned PPs. To ensure consistency between these two documents, simply copy-and-paste the following from the PP to the ST:

- TOE type
- Security problem definition
- Security objectives
- Statement of security requirements

Security Problem Definition

The *Security Problem Definition* section of the ST is designed to describe the security problem(s) that are addressed by the TOE. This definition is accomplished by describing the threats, organizational security policies, and assumptions.

Threats

The security problem definition describes all of the threats in terms of a threat agent, an asset, and an adverse action. If the ST claims conformance to a PP, the ST must include all of the threats from the PP – again, copy-and-paste from the PP to the ST.

Organizational Security Policies

The security problem definition will also include the *organizational security policies* (OSP) including any from the PP with which the ST is claiming conformance. The OSP's are rules and guidelines the TOE must follow.

Assumptions

Any assumptions about the operational environment of the TOE will be included in this section of the ST. This is here to ensure that customers deploy the TOE in an appropriate IT environment matching the assumptions. Once again, if the ST is claiming compliance to a PP, the assumptions from the PP must be carried over to the ST.

Security Objectives

The Security Objectives section of the ST describes how the security objectives will counter the identified threats to the TOE and how the organizational security policies will be met by the TOE. This section will also describe the security objectives of the TOE operational environment and how the operational environment assumptions will be met.

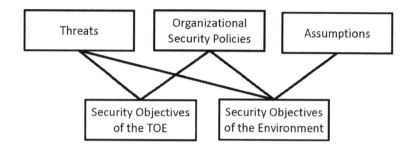

Figure 11: Threats, Policies, Assumptions

As illustrated in Figure 11, each *security objective* for the TOE shall be traced back to:

1. Threats countered by that security objective and
2. OSP's enforced by that security objective

Each security objective of the operational environment shall be traced to:

1. Threats countered by that security objective
2. OSP's enforced by that security objective, and
3. Assumptions upheld by that security objective.

The evaluator will check to see that all threats are countered, all OSP's are upheld, and all assumptions are upheld.

Extended Components Definition

If there are any extended functional or assurance components included in this ST, they all must be clearly described in this section. Extended components are those customized components that are not found within the CC standards Parts 2 or 3. According to CC Part 1, extended components may be used when:

1. CC Part 2 SFRs are inadequate to address the stated security objectives for the TOE
2. CC Part 3 SARs do not cover applicable third-party requirements such as local laws

148

The extended components definition shall describe how each extended component is related to the existing CC components, families, and classes and using a similar model for presentation.

As I had mentioned earlier, I am personally not a fan of extended (or explicitly-stated) requirements because they detract from the notion of an international standard. The use of extended components can be too easily misused to describe product security functions that are "unique" in the marketplace and would serve only to make it more difficult for customers to compare competing products. My belief is that if there is a strong need for an extended component, then it should be submitted as an amendment to the CC standards using the standard process.

Security Requirements

The *Security Requirements* section is used for evaluations at EAL 2 and above. These requirements (SFRs and SARs) are to be clearly defined in this section of the ST.

This section defines and describes the SFRs from CC Part 2 and SARs from CC Part 3 that are claimed in this ST. These SFRs and SARs are selected from the standard set of components from CC Parts 2 and 3. The descriptions can be copied and pasted into this section completing any iteration, assignment, selection and refinement operations in the components as they are satisfied by the TOE.

Security Functional Requirements

In the ST, you claim the SFRs from CC Part 2 that your TOE supports. The SFRs you select depend upon what security features are part of the product you want to evaluate. In the many CC evaluations I have managed and from a number of STs I've examined, I developed a set of "commonly used" SFRs that a novice may use as a starting point if you don't know which SFRs to include in your ST. Table 20 summarizes these "commonly used" SFRs. Of course, if you are claiming conformance with a PP, you must list all of the SFRs from the PP.

Security Functional Class	Functional Components	Description
Security Audit	FAU_ARP.1	Security alarms
	FAU_GEN.1	Alarm generation
	FAU_SAA.1	Audit analysis
	FAU_SAR.1	Audit review
User Data Protection	FDP_IFC.1	Subset information flow control
	FDP_IFF.1	Simple security attributes
Identification and Authentication	FIA_UAU.2	User authentication before any action
	FIA_UID.1	Timing of identification
Security Management	FMT_MOF.1	Management of security function behavior
	FMT_MSA.1	Management of security attributes
	FMT_MSA.3	Static attribute initialization
	FMT_SMF.1	Specification of management functions
	FMT_SMR.1	Security roles

Table 20: Commonly Used SFRs

I have found that product developers don't think extensively about the breadth of security features their products contain. To stimulate their thinking and to elicit ideas for SFRs to include in the ST, I have developed a "standard" set of questions to ask the product developers about their product. These questions highlight SFRs that may be included in the ST.

- Security alarm
    - What kind of alarms does the product produce?
    - Under what conditions are alarms made?
- Audit data generation
    - What kind of audit data does the product collect?
    - What data is collected in audit records?
    - What functions/events are audited?
- Audit analysis
    - What rules are applied to audit records to detect possible violations?
- Audit review
    - What can the user/administrator review from the audit logs?
    - How does the user/administrator review the logs?
- Subset Information flow control

- o What user data flow controls are available for given security policies/roles?
  - o What is the difference between authenticated users and unauthenticated users?
- Simple security attributes
  - o What user data attributes are subject to FDP_IFC.1 requirements?
- User authentication before any action
  - o Are users authenticated before they can perform any action?
  - o How are they authenticated?
- Timing of identification
  - o Does the product require that users identify themselves before allowing any action?
  - o What actions are available to users before identification occurs?
- Management of security functions behavior
  - o What functions are restricted based on users' roles?
  - o To what degree are they restricted?
- Management of security functions
  - o How does the product enforce the behaviors in FMT_MOF.1?
- Static attributes initialization
  - o Does the product provide default values for the attributes in FMT_MSA.1?
  - o Can the user change these defaults?
- Specification of management functions
  - o What security management functions can users perform?
- Security roles
  - o What user roles are there?
  - o What are the differences in the roles?

Security Assurance Requirements

Generally speaking CC evaluations are conducted against one of the standard *Evaluation Assurance Levels* (EAL) rather than a set of (arbitrary) SAR from CC Part 3. My opinion is that the novice should base their first CC evaluation on EAL 2 or at least use it as a starting point. I would expect most mature, commercial product vendors to have established the capabilities to meet the EAL 2 requirements. Also, since most commercial vendors have processes in place to address defects discovered by customers, I suggest augmenting EAL 2 with ALC_FLR.1

(flaw remediation). Table 21 summarizes the assurance requirements for EAL 2 plus basic flaw remediation.

Security Assurance Class	Assurance Components	Description
Development	ADV_ARC.1	Security architecture description
	ADV_FSP.2	Security-enforcing functional specification
	ADV_TDS.1	Basic design
Guidance Documents	AGD_OPE.1	Operational user guidance
	AGD_PRE.1	Preparative guidance
Life-Cycle Support	ALC_CMC.2	Use of a CM system
	ALC_CMS.2	Parts of the TOE CM coverage
	ALC_DEL.1	Delivery procedures
	ALC_FLR.1	Basic flaw remediation
Tests	ATE_COV.1	Evidence of coverage
	ATE_FUN.1	Functional testing
	ATE_IND.2	Independent testing - simple
Vulnerability Assessment	AVA_VAN.2	Vulnerability analysis

Table 21: EAL 2 Augemented with ALC_FLR.1 Requirements

This section of the ST describes the EAL selected for the evaluation and each SAR within that EAL. The individual SARs can be copied and pasted from the CC Part 3 to the ST.

Security Requirements Rationale

This section of the ST provides a clear illustration that all of the stated TOE Security Objectives are met by the claimed Security Functional Requirements (SFR). Typically, this illustration is done by using a matrix with TOE Security Objectives listed on one axis and SFRs on the other. This section of the ST must not only show how the SFRs meet all of the TOE Security Objectives, it must also show that all of the SFRs are mapped to at least one TOE Security Objective.

In addition to delivering the rationale for the SFRs, this section of the ST explains why the selected Security Assurance Requirements (SAR) were chosen. This usually amounts to a statement that the selected EAL (and the associated SARs) meet the desired and expected level of assurance.

TOE Summary Specification

To me, the *TOE Summary Specification* (TSS) section is the most readable section for the layman (e.g. customers). This summarizes the security functional and assurance claims and is easier for an end-user to read and understand simply because it tends to use more descriptive product language rather than Common Criteria jargon.

The TSS describes the features of the product and how they meet the functional requirements from the user's perspective. That is, it describes how users can use the product in the secure, evaluated configuration. While this is intended to be a high-level description, users can see what security claims are met and how. Evaluators will examine the TSS to ensure that the narrative descriptions of the product security features are consistent with the SFRs.

Examples STs

The appendix entitled Recent Evaluations at the end of this book contains a list of products that completed evaluations using the CC 3.1 standards. This list was compiled from information found on the Common Criteria Portal website [CC Portal] in April 2010. The Common Criteria Portal also has pointers to ST documents for each of the certified products. These references may be useful as examples of what other vendors have claimed and how evaluated ST documents are organized and the level of detail contained in them.

Chapter 11: Development Evidence

After the Security Target (ST) document, the next major set of CC evidence documents is the *Development* evidence. Development evidence is essentially product design documentation; evaluators will examine this evidence to verify vendor security functional claims. According to the *Common Evaluation Methodology* standard (CEM) [CC Standards], the purpose of the development evaluation activity is to assess the design documentation in support of understanding how the *TOE security functions* (TSF) meet the *security functional requirements* (SFR). This understanding is derived from examining the development evidence documentation which consists of functional specifications, TOE design description, implementation description (e.g. source code), and a security architecture description. For the higher assurance evaluations, internal descriptions and security policy model descriptions are also required. The *Development* assurance class (ADV) evidence requirements vary depending on the EAL.

For most product developers, functional specifications, internal designs, and architecture documents are normal outputs of the product design phase. I have found that while these documents exist, they are either out-of-date or they do not highlight the security aspects of the product. Moreover, they don't necessarily correlate to the content requirements of the respective CC assurance documents, especially given that the content of the ST feeds the details here. It is that up-to-date, CC evaluation-focused design documentation that the CC evaluator will need to successfully complete the ADV evaluation. Product developers certainly are encouraged to leverage any and all existing development documents including external design specifications, internal design specifications, and architecture descriptions to generate the ADV evidence. Some vendors that have a great deal of experience with CC have integrated the CC evidence development into their normal product development cycles.

In this chapter, we will discuss the different *Development* (ADV) evidence requirements for EAL 1 through 4. The ADV families are:

- Functional Specifications (ADV_FSP)
- Security Architecture (ADV_ARC)
- TOE Design (ADV_TDS)
- Implementation Representation (ADV_IMP)
- TSF Internals (ADV_INT)
- Security Policy Modeling (ADV_SPM)

For me, one of the benefits of hiring a CC consultant to create the *Development* evidence is that software product developers think of their code in terms of programs, subroutines, data stores, Internet connections, and the functions the code performs. Consequently, the design and architecture documentation that typically come from developers describe how programs and subroutines interact to perform a function. *Development* evidence is oriented toward security functions and their logical interfaces. The CC consultant can "translate" the developer descriptions into concepts and terms the CC evaluator can understand. CC consultants I've worked with have gathered the developer design documents and interviewed developers to pull together the information they need to complete the *Development* evidence. While some would argue that vendors do not have to hire expensive CC consultants to create evidence documents and that developer documentation should suffice, I would argue that CC evaluators would be hard-pressed to get the kind of information they need from much of the "normal" developer documentation.

On a personal note, I always had difficulty differentiating the physical and logical models of the TOE. Perhaps because I'm more of an engineer than a computer scientist (in spite of my formal education), I relate better to things on a physical scale. Figure 12 shows how the physical model and logical model describe the same TOE, just from different perspectives. The TOE, in fact is both a physical set of hardware, software and documentation as well as a logical collection of security functions (TSF). The *Development* evidence, including the functional specifications and the TOE design, describe the logical model of the TOE. While I like to think of (software) products as a set of code modules (e.g. data base access routines or communications code), the *Development* evidence describes functions such as security audit, security management, identification, and authentication. The *Development* evidence discusses interfaces to these security functions. These *TOE Security Function Interfaces* (TSFI) can be things like user login, reports, settings and status. The *Functional Specifications* (FSP) take a step toward satisfying my need to connect to the physical world by providing a mapping of TSF to TOE implementation describing how the TOE performs the security function.

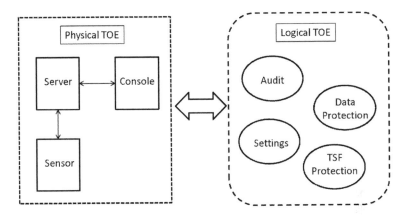

Figure 12: Physical vs. Logical TOE

Functional Specifications

Most software developers are familiar with the concept of *functional specifications* (FSP) as high-level descriptions of the product functions. In CC evaluations, FSP are focused on the security functions claimed in the ST. According to CC Part 3, the objective of the *Functional Specifications* family (ADV_FSP) is to describe the TSFI. These are the interfaces to the *TOE security function* (TSF) that are within the TOE, but outside of the TSF. The interfaces are inputs, outputs and services from the TSF. For example, a database accepts SQL queries as inputs from a client applet, performs the operations, and returns responses. The FSP describe the SQL queries and the returned responses, but there are no descriptions of how the inputs are processed or communicated – these are part of the TOE design (ADV_TDS).

You should be aware of some special terminology used throughout the ADV class descriptions in CC Part 3. The first sets of terms classify the different types of interfaces as:

- *SFR-enforcing* – an interface that can be traced directly to a SFR
- *SFR-supporting* – an interface that supports the TOE security policies
- *SFR-non-interfering* – an interface where no SFR-enforcing functionality has any dependence

As the assurance levels increases, you will need to provide greater description and proof that the interface fits the designated category. Each TSFI is described in terms of its:

1. *Purpose* – general goal of the interface
2. *Method of use* – how the interface is to be used
3. *Parameters* – inputs and outputs
4. *Parameter descriptions* - meaningful descriptions
5. *Actions* – what the interface does
6. *Error message descriptions* – what generates the error, error messages and error code definitions

I will discuss the first four ADV_FSP classes covering the requirements for EAL 1-4 since these will be most commonly used by commercial products. The components are:

EAL	Component requirement
EAL 1	ADV_FSP.1 – Basic functional specification
EAL 2	ADV_FSP.2 – Security-enforcing functional specification
EAL 3	ADV_FSP.3 – Functional specification with complete summary
EAL 4	ADV_FSP.4 – Complete functional specification

ADV_FSP.1, *Basic Functional Specifications*, requires a description of the purpose and method of use for each *SFR-enforcing* and *SFR-supporting* interface. It also requires a mapping to the related SFRs.

ADV_FSP.2, *Security-Enforcing Functional Specifications*, expands on the requirements of ADV_FSP.1 by requiring the description of the purpose and method of use for all TSFIs. In addition, descriptions of the actions and error message descriptions for all of the *SFR-enforcing* functions of the TSFI must be provided. ADV_FSP.2 and above are dependent on ADV_TDS.1.

ADV_FSP.3, *Functional Specification with Complete Summary*, requires in addition to the requirements from ADV_FSP.2 descriptions of

SFR-enforcing actions and exceptions associated with invoking the TSFI. ADV_FSP.3 also requires a summary of the *SFR-supporting* and *SFR-non-interfering* actions of each TSFI.

ADV_FSP.4, *Complete Functional Specifications*, requires a complete description of the TSFI including: purpose, method of use, all parameters, all actions, and all error messages.

Security Architecture

The purpose of the *security architecture* (ADV_ARC) is to provide evidence to support the claims of the TSF. The developer is expected to describe the TOE design and implementation illustrating that the TSF cannot be bypassed or tampered. Domain separation will also be described in the security architecture. There is only one component in this family ADV_ARC.1 and it depends on ADV_FSP.1 and ADV_TDS.1.

EAL	Component requirement
EAL 1	None
EAL 2 - 4	ADV_ARC.1 – Security architecture description

The first requirement of ADV_ARC.1, *Security Architecture Description*, is that the security architecture descriptions are consistent with the level of *SFR-enforcing* functions described in the TOE design. This will require consistency with evidence for ADV_TDS.1. All of the modules listed in the security architecture must also be included in the either the functional specifications or the TOE design evidence.

Some TOE security functions maintain environments for external entities such as operating systems providing application memory space. Descriptions of these security domains must be included in the security architecture. Descriptions of how these environments are maintained and kept separate by the TSF will be included in the security architecture.

It is expected that the TSF is initialized in a secure state. All of the components involved in the secure initialization process must be described in the security architecture. Sufficient description must be provided so that the evaluator can determine which components are invoked and that the initialization process is secure.

Self-protection is a key element of the security architecture and refers to the ability of the TSF to prevent manipulation from external entities from unauthorized modification. Self-protection mechanisms may be physical or logical restrictions. It may also include the notion of privilege and domain separation.

Another key characteristic of the security architecture is the ability to prevent bypassing the security functions. For example, a user must not be able to use any protected TOE functions without first identifying and authenticating him/herself to the TOE. The evaluator will need to rely on not only the security architecture to determine non-bypassability but will also need to examine the functional specifications, TOE design, and other evidence. The evaluator is obligated to ensure that each TSFI is analyzed against all claimed SFRs. A matrix of SFRs versus TSFI would be handy to include here.

TOE Design

The *TOE Design* (ADV_TDS) introduces some more special terminology. *Subsystems* are considered parts of the architecture. They are the "bigger blocks" in the block diagram of the architecture. *Modules* are "smaller blocks" and perform specific functions. The goal of the TOE design is to describe the TSF boundary and how the TSF implements the SFRs. *Subsystems* and *modules* are categorized as *SFR-enforcing, SFR-supporting* or *SFR-non-interfering*. As expected, as the level of assurance increases, the level of detail increases from subsystem- to module-level.

EAL	Component requirement
EAL 2	ADV_TDS.1 – Basic design
EAL 3	ADV_TDS.2 – Architectural design
EAL 4	ADV_TDS.3 – Basic modular design

As with the ADV_FSP, I will discuss the *TOE Design* requirements for EAL 2 to 4 only.

ADV_TDS.1, *TOE Design*, requires a description of the basic design structure of the TOE using *subsystems*. All of the *subsystems* within the TSF will be listed along with a description of the behavior and interactions of all *SFR-enforcing* subsystems. The behavior of *SFR-supporting* and *SFR-non-interfering* subsystems will be included as well just to demonstrate that they are not *SFR-enforcing*.

ADV_TDS.2, *Architectural Design*, documentation will add to ADV_TDS.1 more detailed descriptions of *SFR-supporting* and *SFR-non-interfering* subsystems. There should be sufficient details provided about the behavior and interactions of these subsystems such that the evaluator can verify their classification.

ADV_TDS.3, *Basic Modular Design*, evidence goes to the module-level of detail. The TOE design is explained in terms of *modules* as well as *subsystems*. All *modules* must be mapped to their *subsystem*. Each *SFR-enforcing module* will be described in terms of its purpose, interfaces and interactions. Each *SFR-supporting* and *SFR-non-interfering module* will be described by its purpose and interaction with other *modules*.

Implementation Representation

Implementation representation (ADV_IMP) is only applicable at EAL 4 and above. The *implementation representation* may take the form of software or firmware source code, hardware diagrams, and IC diagrams. The key to ADV_IMP is the mapping between the implementation representation and the TOE design of the TSF.

Many product vendors are concerned with this requirement in terms of protecting *intellectual property* (IP) and adhering to corporate (or government) regulations regarding the handling and protection of certain sensitive IP. It is prudent to check with your company's legal department and executive staff to determine what restrictions might apply to the exposure of the IP contained in the implementation representation evidence. I have had to deal with business unit vice presidents who would not allow source code to be exposed to CC evaluation labs and would not allow the source code to be examined off-site. Some of the products I've dealt with contained cryptographic software. Some cryptographic algorithms and code are export-restricted and subject to U.S. export laws. These issues had to be discussed with our legal department.

The other issue with software source code is that although the CC evaluation is focused on the TOE, the source code usually is not; it is generally not practical to try to separate out the TOE source code from the rest of the product code. This may pose a problem if evaluators stumble upon a vulnerability in a part of the product that is not part of the TOE. While technically this should not be an issue, I have run into situations where it caused us to stop and think about it.

Chapter 12: Lifecycle Support Evidence

The purpose of the evaluation of lifecycle support evidence is to assess the vendor's security procedures during development and support of the TOE. The *Lifecycle Support* (ALC) assurance class covers a fairly wide range of activities from configuration management (software people call this source code control) to delivery.

As with the evidence used in the *Development* assurance class, much of the *Lifecycle Support* evidence can be derived directly from what I would consider "normal" documentation for any commercial product vendor. Most commercial vendors would certainly have procedures in place to address the ALC requirements simply because other business considerations such as business continuity, customer demand, and engineering efficiency would require it. How much actual written documentation is available to draw upon to generate the ALC evidence depends on the vendor.

In this chapter, we will focus on the requirements for EAL 1 through 4 which cover the following topics:

- Configuration management (CM) capabilities (ALC_CMC)
- CM scope (ALC_CMS)
- Delivery (ALC_DEL)
- Development security (ALC_DVS)
- Flaw remediation (ALC_FLR)
- Lifecycle definition (ALC_LCD)
- Tools and techniques (ALC_TAT)

CM Capabilities

A mark of a mature development organization is their use of a *configuration management* (CM) system and associated procedures; they recognize that without them, any large product development effort can spin out of control thus opening up the possibilities for vulnerabilities to be introduced. The objectives for ALC_CMC are:

1. Ensure that the TOE is correct and complete before it is sent to the customer
2. Ensure that no configuration items are missing during evaluation

3. Prevent unauthorized modification, addition or deletion of TOE configuration items

As the assurance level increases, ALC_CMC components add specific requirements to the CM system. These requirements are intended to increase the likelihood that errors and malicious modifications will be prevented.

EAL	Component requirement
EAL 1	ALC_CMC.1 – Labeling of the TOE
EAL 2	ALC_CMC.2 – Use of a CM system
EAL 3	ALC_CMC.3 – Authorization controls
EAL 4	ALC_CMC.4 – Production support, acceptance procedures, and automation

ALC_CMC.1, *Labeling of the TOE*, requires just a unique labeling of the TOE to remove any ambiguity as to what version is being evaluated. This reference should coincide with the label given to the TOE in the *Security Target* (ST) document.

ALC_CMC.2, *Use of a CM System*, also requires a unique *TOE label* and adds the requirement of the use of a CM system to uniquely identify all of the configuration items in the TOE. The developer is to provide the CM system and CM documentation to the evaluator for this part of the evaluation. The CM documentation should describe how all of the configuration items are uniquely identified and how each version is to be tracked.

ALC_CMC.3, *Authorization Controls*, examines the CM system authorization and access controls. This component adds to the ALC_CMC.2 evaluation of the CM system access controls. Access controls on the CM system will help prevent unauthorized modifications to the TOE configuration items. The CM documentation will include a CM plan with the following:

*   TOE development activities subject to the CM procedures
*   Applicable tools and forms to be used
*   CM tools operation guidance
*   Items under CM system control
*   Roles and responsibilities
*   Description of change management
*   Other CM procedures

All configuration items must be maintained in accordance with the CM plan. In my experience, vendors are expected to provide specifics about the CM software used (e.g. CVS version 1.12.13) and the user manual. Evaluators may also ask where the server that houses the CM system is located and on what platform it is running.

ALC_CMC.4, *Production Support, Acceptance Procedures, and Automation*, requires greater automation to prevent human errors. Evaluators will be examining evidence to ensure that automation is used to prevent unauthorized modifications to the TOE and TOE configuration items. You can expect evaluators to want to do their examination for this assurance component in-person, so an on-site visit would be necessary.

CM Scope

Configuration Management Scope (ALC_CMS) evidence describes what is managed by the configuration management (CM) system. For software developers, CM systems generally manage the source code. The table below summarizes the ALC_CMS requirements based on EAL.

EAL	Component requirement
EAL 1	ALC_CMS.1 –TOE CM coverage
EAL 2	ALC_CMS.2 – Parts of the TOE CM coverage
EAL 3	ALC_CMS.3 – Implementation representation CM coverage
EAL 4	ALC_CMS.4 – Problem tracking CM coverage

ALC_CMS.1, *TOE CM Coverage*, requires that not only is the TOE (product) controlled by the CM system but the CC evidence documents are also managed and protected by the CM system and procedures.

ALC_CMS.2, *Parts of the TOE CM Coverage*, requires that all parts of the TOE are included in the CM coverage; this includes the TOE, the parts that comprise the TOE, and the CC evidence documentation. The configuration list will uniquely identify each item and its developer (organization).

ALC_CMS.3, *Implementation Representation CM Coverage*, adds to ALC_CMS.2 the requirement that the TOE implementation representation is included in the CM coverage. This means holding the TOE source code under CM system control. To me, this is a natural thing for any developer to do – if they use a source code management system at all.

ALC_CMS.4, *Problem Tracking CM Coverage*, introduces the requirement that problem (defect) tracking is added to the CM coverage.

In my experience, defect tracking systems are separate from the CM system although some have linkages between them. The requirement here is that security flaw reports are to be included in the configuration list. Security flaw reports and resolutions associated with the TOE are to be managed by the CM system and procedures.

Delivery

ALC_DEL.1, *Delivery Procedures*, is the only assurance component in this family for all EALs. The purpose of this component is to describe the all of the procedures used to ensure the secure distribution and delivery of the TOE to the end customer.

EAL	Component requirement
EAL 1 - 4	ALC_DEL.1 – Delivery procedures

Collecting and developing documentation on all of the procedures used to distribute and deliver the TOE may surprisingly prove to be a challenge for large product development organizations. There may be multiple delivery mechanisms such as delivery as a pre-packaged appliance (e.g. customized hardware bundled with software), software-only (in the form of a CD or DVD), or electronic delivery over the Internet. Each of these delivery mechanisms may, in turn, have multiple parties (both internal and external) involved. We outsourced some of its product disk duplication and distribution functions to third-parties. We had to obtain the documented procedures from each of them to complete the CC evidence for this assurance component. Product packaging procedures for physical media should also demonstrate how they secure the TOE.

Secure electronic delivery measures may include the use of cryptography (e.g. checksums and digital signatures). Details of any cryptography used will need to be documented to demonstrate how it protects the TOE.

Development Security

Development Security (ALC_DVS) evidence describes the security measures taken to protect the development process.

EAL	Component requirement
EAL 1 & 2	None
EAL 3 & 4	ALC_DVS.1 – Identification of security measures

ALC_DVS.1, *Identification of Security Measures*, requires that the developer provide development security documentation that describes the physical, procedural and personnel security measures taken to protect the security of the TOE development process.

For most commercial product vendors, the protections put in place by corporate facilities and safety departments are the basis for the evidence needed to meet the *Development Security* requirements. These measures and procedures are usually documented and most employees are trained on these measures by law. This includes personnel access to development sites and restricted development areas (e.g. labs), transfer of intellectual property, and access revocation procedures.

Evidence should document how employees and contractors are granted access to the development areas, who is responsible for granting and revoking access, how visitors are admitted and escorted through the facility, and what background checks are made on new employees.

According to the CEM, a site visit by the evaluator is mandatory to evaluate this requirement. They will need to see that the documented procedures are being followed. They will want to see the procedures "in action."

Flaw Remediation

Curiously, none of the EALs require any component of the *Flaw Remediation* (ALC_FLR) family although CC Part 3 defines 3 components. The purpose of this assurance family is to ensure that the TOE security will be maintained over time. Commercial product vendors generally provide on-going support to all of their customers in the form of up-grades and bug fixes; so in my opinion, most any commercial product vendor should be able to meet the requirements of at least one of the ALC_FLR components. You will find that many vendors do augment their EAL claims with a component from ALC_FLR.

The description of ALC_FLR in CC Part 3 acknowledges that any modification to the evaluated TOE including "security bug fixes" makes the TOE "unevaluated" because it changes the TOE. This may be a reason why components in this family are not required at any EAL.

Component	Description
ALC_FLR.1	Basic flaw remediation
ALC_FLR.2	Flaw reporting procedures
ALC_FLR.3	Systematic flaw remediation

ALC_FLR.1, *Basic Flaw Remediation,* requires that flaw remediation procedures describe:

- How security flaws in the TOE are tracked
- Security flaw reports include the nature of the flaw and status of the remediation
- Corrective actions for each security flaw
- How remediation information will be provided to customers

Most commercial product vendors will have in place procedures to handle defect reports from customers. Security defect reports need to be identified separately from non-security issues. All of these procedures need to be documented. Some of these procedures may be performed by departments such as call center support. Customer support will, in many cases, be the first to receive a defect report from a customer. The procedures and systems used by that department must be documented. The procedures for notifying customers (TOE users) once corrective actions (e.g. bug fixes or patches) are ready to be distributed need to be documented.

ALC_FLR.2, *Flaw Reporting Procedures,* adds the requirement for developers to have a process for accepting and acting on security flaw reports from customers. In addition, this component requires that the developer have procedures to ensure that corrections do not introduce new flaws. There must be documented procedures explaining how customers can contact the developer to report security flaws. The flaw remediation procedures must describe how each defect report is handled until a correction is made.

ALC_FLR.3 is called *Systematic Flaw Remediation,* because greater automation is required to ensure timely response to defect reports. Customers may register with the developer to obtain security flaw reports and corrections with specific points of contact.

Lifecycle Definition

The ALC_LCD, *Lifecycle Definition,* evidence describes the developer's product lifecycle.

EAL	Component requirement
EAL 1 & 2	None
EAL 3 & 4	ALC_LCD.1 –Developer-defined lifecycle model

ALC_LCD.1, *Developer-Defined Lifecycle Model*, evidence documents the model that is used for the development and maintenance of the TOE. The documentation for the lifecycle should include the development phases, development procedures, tools and techniques used, and the overall management structure with defined roles and responsibilities.

While the CC does not dictate any particular lifecycle model (e.g. waterfall or agile), the evaluator will examine the model to see that it makes a "positive contribution" to the development and maintenance of the TOE.

Tools and Techniques

The use of development tools such as compilers and testing tools are important for the development of consistent, reliable products. The objective of the *Tools and Techniques* (ALC_TAT) evidence is to document the developer's use of tools.

EAL	Component requirement
EAL 1 – 3	None
EAL 4	ALC_TAT.1 - Well-defined development tools

ALC_TAT.1, *Well-Defined Development Tools*, requires that each development tool is *well-defined*. The CEM gives the example of a *well-defined* programming language as one that follows the ISO standard with a clear and complete syntax. Also, any implementation-dependent options and the effect they have on the tool's output must be described. This refers to things such as compiling or linking options.

Chapter 13: Tests, Vulnerability Assessment and Guidance Evidence

Tests Evidence

The purpose of the evaluation of the *Tests* assurance class (ATE) evidence is to confirm that the TOE security functions perform as designed. This means that the components within the ATE class were designed to have the evaluators confirm the statements made in the other CC evidence such as functional specifications and the Security Target (ST).

This part of the evaluation requires the close involvement of the quality assurance (QA) team members. They will be required to provide information about what was tested and how the product was tested. They may be required to develop additional tests to specifically test the security functions as defined by the ST and *Functional Specifications* (FSP).

In this chapter, we will focus on the requirements for EAL 1 through 4 only for the ATE class with the following topics:

- Coverage (ATE_COV)
- Depth (ATE_DPT)
- Functional test (ATE_FUN)
- Independent test (ATE_IND)

Coverage

Test Coverage (ATE_COV) evidence describes the breadth of test coverage performed by developers across the TOE module interfaces.

EAL	Component
EAL 1	None
EAL 2	ATE_COV.1 - Evidence of coverage
EAL 3 & 4	ATE_COV.2 - Analysis of coverage

The objective of ATE_COV.1, *Evidence of Coverage,* is to demonstrate that some of the *TOE security function interfaces* (TSFI) have been tested. The developer must illustrate how some of the tests correspond to the interfaces defined in the functional specifications. A mapping between SFR, TSFI, test details and test results would provide the kind of evidence the evaluator can easily review.

ATE_COV.2, *Analysis of Coverage*, expands on ATE_COV.1 to cover all TSFIs. The mapping must include all of the TSFIs found in the FSP. In my experience, evaluators are looking for specific tests that clearly exercise the TSFIs. During normal QA testing, sometimes the test suites do not explicitly test the security functions claimed in the ST. In this case, the QA team may need to develop, run and record tests to provide complete coverage of all TSFIs.

Depth

The objective of *Depth* testing (ATE_DPT) is to examine the depth of testing conducted by the developer. More detailed design documentation is required to conduct this analysis, so the dependencies include architecture, TOE design and functional test evidence.

EAL	Component requirement
EAL 1 - 2	None
EAL 3 & 4	ATE_DPT.1 – Basic design testing

For ATE_DPT.1, *Basic Design Testing*, the developer will provide an analysis of the depth of testing. This analysis will include correspondence between the tests and the TSF subsystems in the TOE design. It will also illustrate that all subsystems have been tested. The test documentation should include the test plan, test setup, test steps, expected results, and actual results. The evaluator will examine the test evidence against expected behavior according to the design documentation.

Functional Tests

Functional Test (ATE_FUN) evidence documents the tests performed by the developer on security functions claimed in the ST.

EAL	Component requirement
EAL 1	None
EAL 2 - 4	ATE_FUN.1 – Functional test

The ATE_FUN.1, *Functional Test*, evidence requires the developer to test the TSF and record the results. The test documentation will include the test plan, expected and actual test results. The test plans will describe the test setup and steps required to run the tests. Of course, the actual test results must correspond to the expected test results. Test setup information must be detailed enough for tests to be duplicated with identical results. Evaluators will re-run a sampling of the developer's functional tests to verify the results. If tests must be run in a particular order (e.g. to set up pre-conditions for other tests), then this order must be well-documented.

Independent Test

Independent testing (ATE_IND) is intended to provide greater assurance over developer testing. Independent testing is developed and performed by the evaluators.

EAL	Component requirement
EAL 1	ATE_IND.1 – Independent test
EAL 2 - 4	ATE_IND.2 – Independent testing - Sample

ATE_IND.1, *Independent Testing,* merely requires that the TOE is made available for evaluator testing. The evaluator will develop an independent test plan and execute a subset of tests on the TOE security functionality.

Independent Testing – Sample, ATE_IND.2, requires the developer to provide an equivalent test environment so that the evaluator can run a subset of the developer's tests. It may be convenient to have the evaluator run these tests during their on-site visit allowing him/her access to the developer's test environment. This eliminates the logistical issues of shipping hardware to the evaluator's lab and avoids the complications of trying to replicate the test system configuration to the developer's specifications.

Vulnerability Assessment Evidence

The objective of *Vulnerability Assessment* is to determine if vulnerabilities discovered during development or evaluation could be exploited. Exploitation of these vulnerabilities might lead to unauthorized exposure of data or other circumvention of security functions. There is only one family in this class; it is AVA_VAN, *Vulnerability Analysis.* As EAL 1 through 4 is the focus of this book, I will discuss the 3 components that are required in EAL 1 through 4.

EAL	Component requirement
EAL 1	AVA_VAN.1 – Vulnerability survey
EAL 2 & 3	AVA_VAN.2 – Vulnerability analysis
EAL 4	AVA_VAN.3 – Focused vulnerability analysis

Component AVA_VAN.1, *Vulnerability Survey*, requires that the developer conduct a survey of vulnerability information found in the public domain that may apply to the TOE. The evaluator will perform penetration tests to confirm that these vulnerabilities cannot be exploited to expose the TOE to risk. These public sources of vulnerability information can be websites such as:

- U.S. Computer Emergency Readiness Team
- Mitre Common Vulnerabilities and Exposures
- U.S. Department of Homeland Security/U.S.-CERT National Vulnerability Database
- SecurityFocus Vulnerability Database

The developer will also provide information demonstrating why these vulnerabilities are not exploitable in the TOE and operational environment.

AVA_VAN.2, *Vulnerability Analysis*, adds to the AVA_VAN.1 requirements with an evaluator-developed penetration testing suite. The evaluator will use information from the functional specifications, TOE design and security architecture to uncover potential vulnerabilities. The evaluator will then perform penetration tests to attempt to exploit those vulnerabilities. If any of these vulnerabilities are exploitable, this portion of the evaluation fails.

AVA_VAN.3, *Focused Vulnerability Analysis*, increases the depth of the evaluator penetration testing by using the implementation representation along with the functional specifications, design and architecture documentation. The attack potential (i.e. anticipated knowledge of the attacker) increases from *Basic* to *Enhanced-Basic*.

Guidance Evidence

The AGD, *Guidance* class refers to user documentation delivered with the product. These are typically user manuals, administrator guides, and installation and setup manuals. One of the major security issues identified by SANS and OWASP [OWASP] is insecurely configured products. Providing proper instructions to users on how to securely set up, install and configure products can address this set of serious issues.

EAL	Component requirement
EAL 1 - 4	AGD_OPE.1 - Operational guidance
EAL 1 - 4	AGD_PRE.1 – Preparative guidance

There are two families in this class - each having only one component. These components recognize the different roles users have in the installation and operation of the TOE. All user roles must be accounted for in the AGD evidence.

AGD_OPE.1, *Operational Guidance*, describes to the user the security functionality of the TOE. The *Operational Guidance* must describe role-specific functions and privileges. For each interface, the *Operational Guidance* must include descriptions of:

- Methods users can use to invoke the functions (e.g. command-line or system call)
- Parameters that can be set by the user along with secure values
- Responses or error codes

All relevant security event types must be documented in the *Operational Guidance* for each user role. Users need to know what security events may occur and what to do in order to remain secure. Similarly, users need to know all possible modes of operation and the implications they have on security. Evaluators will review guidance evidence to ensure that it is clear and reasonable.

ADG_PRE.1, *Preparative Guidance*, provides information to users on how to securely install and configure the TOE. *Preparative Guidance* begins with secure acceptance directions in accordance with the developer's secure delivery process. This must be consistent with the evidence presented for ALC_DEL. The installation descriptions must include direction on securing the operational environment. These should include:

- Minimum system requirements
- Requirements of the operational environment
- Steps to securely configure the TOE
- Directions for changing installation security settings of the TOE
- How to handle exceptions and problems

Guidance evidence can be delivered as addendums to standard product documentation to the end-user or can be integrated into the standard user guidance. In either case, the objective is to give the customers information about how to securely install, configure and operate the product in accordance with the evaluation conditions.

PART 4: STORIES FROM THE TRENCHES

In this part:

Chapter 14: Success Stories

Regardless of whether your goal is to merely meet a government procurement requirement or to begin a journey toward improving product security, it is your responsibility to complete these evaluations in a timely and cost-effective manner. This chapter is devoted to reviewing the activities and procedures that I have found lead to the completion of on-time and on-budget CC evaluations.

Best Practices

I have some best practices that have been developed from my many years as a commercial software product development manager and my experience managing CC evaluation projects. Most of these lessons were learned the hard way - by trial-and-error. I have mentioned some of these best practices throughout the book, but in this chapter, I wanted to capture those best practices in one place, share some stories around them, and to share stories I've heard from other vendors and evaluators. My goal is to provide some insights into what makes a CC evaluation go smoothly, efficiently, quickly, and economically for product vendors. The key best practices can be summarized as:

- Meet minimum requirements
- Allocate time
- Minimize changes to the plan
- Reuse certification materials
- Weekly status calls with evaluators
- Dedicated technical writer
- Synchronize evaluation with development

These items represent the "low-hanging fruit" of practices that help ensure the completion of a successful CC evaluation. These are practices that I've found to be most helpful and easiest to implement that have had a direct impact on the success of the CC evaluation project. To further illustrate the utility of these practices and to give you a glimpse into the learning process I went through to determine that these really are useful practices, I will present some vignettes.

Meet Minimum Requirements

In 2006, we completed the CC evaluation for Symantec Critical System Protection (SCSP) at EAL 2. This effort took nearly a year to complete from the time we formally engaged CC consultants until the Scheme validation was completed and the certificate was awarded in November 2006. This CC evaluation was the first for the SCSP development team, although some members of the team had experience with other government evaluation programs from previous jobs. One of the keys to completing this project quickly was the effort we and the CC consultants put into minimizing the security functional requirements claims and the EAL for the evaluation.

Early in our planning discussions, we met with product management and had telephone conversations with our Federal Sales representatives to understand which customers were asking for the CC evaluation; what their expectations were with respect to assurance levels and completion time; what product version they expected to be evaluated; and what product type they considered the product. It turns out that the last question about product type was the critical issue.

SCSP is marketed as a host-based intrusion detection and intrusion prevention system. The U.S. government has several intrusion detection system (IDS) *Protection Profiles* (PP) [NIAP] that are applicable to this product. These PP contain specific *security functional requirements* (SFR) and a specific EAL. In this case, the applicable PP was the *U.S. Government Protection Profile Intrusion Detection System for Basic Robustness Environments*. Within this PP were several SFRs which we deemed would be difficult to demonstrate compliance.

The IDS PP included the requirement FAU_STG.4, *Prevention of Audit Data Loss*. SCSP relied on the environment (operating system file system) to protect the audit data, so SCSP itself could not claim conformance to this requirement. The IDS PP also included FAU_SEL.1, *Selective Audit*, that enables the user to selectively sort and filter audit data records for review. SCSP did not have this functionality nor was this functionality planned to be added to the product. These SFRs and a few others caused us to decide not to pursue evaluation against the IDS PP, but it also meant we would need to carefully select what SFRs we would include in the evaluation.

The process we used to decide which SFRs to include was to use the SFRs in the IDS PP as a starting point, eliminating the ones that did not apply, and then adding a few that we could easily demonstrate compliance. The IDS PP required evaluation at EAL 2 augmented with

ALC_FLR.2, *Flaw Remediation*, but we chose EAL 2 without the augmentation because the SCSP organization was going through some internal changes that affected the evaluation of the flaw remediation processes. While the number of SFRs (21 in total) that were included in this evaluation was significant, the effort to gather, develop and evaluate the evidence was minimized by careful examination of the product features and a clear understanding for the CC requirements.

Even though there were some competitors claiming to pursue evaluations against the IDS PP, we decided to take a path that would minimize our risk of failure. We believed that if we would have a difficult time meeting some of the SFRs in the IDS PP, so would our competitors. As it turned out, no competitor completed evaluation against the IDS PP until 2009.

Allocate Time

In Chapter 6: Resource Allocation, we discussed who is involved in the CC project and how much time they can expect to spend during the project. One of the first questions I get from every development manager is, "How long is this going to take?" This is certainly the case with teams new to the CC evaluation process. One of the exceptions to this was the Symantec Enterprise Firewall (SEF) team.

SEF was the first Symantec product to complete a CC evaluation and in 2002 was one of the first in the world to certify a product against the U.S. Department of Defense *Application-Level Firewall Protection Profile for Basic Robustness Environments* – although a dispute caused the claim to be revoked. This same product development team went on to successfully complete 5 CC evaluations – several at EAL 4. Much of their success can be attributed to allocating the time necessary to efficiently complete the CC evaluation project.

The product development team learned through experience how long it would take to complete their respective tasks during the CC evaluation. They knew how long it would take to develop the necessary design documents to satisfy the development evaluation requirements. They learned what additional test scripts would have to be designed, executed and recorded to meet the CC test evaluation requirements. Moreover, the team members had become comfortable with what they each needed to do and were able to build this effort into their individual and project work schedules.

I will give a great deal of credit to Regina Hammond, the program manager who led these CC evaluation projects for the SEF and

Gateway Security (SGS) products. She learned what was expected of the team and put in place task lists and project plans that meshed with all of the other demands placed on the product team members (e.g. new product releases and bug fixes). This ability turned out to be quite valuable as there were many occasions when emergencies would arise and personnel would need to be assigned to higher-priority projects. Having Regina anticipate the evaluation project needs and manage the resource allocations with a global view of all of the activities in the department helped minimize disruptions in the CC evaluation project.

Minimize Changes To The Plan

One of the major reasons why I want to see CC evaluations be completed as quickly as possible is because the CC evaluation process is all about evaluating a static view of the TOE (product). Changes to the product will force the re-evaluation of some of the evidence that has already been evaluated. In a business environment where change is rapid and constant, the CC evaluation project team is challenged to stay on course. On many occasions I have had to resist attempts to change the product version or include a new feature or add a supported platform to the evaluation.

Changing things in the product under evaluation that may outwardly seem simple can significantly delay progress. Changes to the product, including the version number will force the evaluator to go back through all of the evidence s/he has already evaluated to see what impact the change has on the evidence and on his/her evaluation verdicts. This is extra work and takes time.

Symantec acquired On Technologies in early 2004. One of its flagship products, iCommand, was capable of remotely provisioning (distributing) computer systems with a variety of software including operating systems and applications.

There was a large (surprisingly, non-government) customer demanding CC evaluation on this product. The product development team knew they were about to undertake some major product changes along with a name change as part of the transition after the company acquisition. We decided to delay the start of the CC evaluation effort until the product release plan was finalized for the newly-named Symantec LiveState Delivery (LSD) version 6.0 product. The contract with the CC evaluation lab was signed in November 2004.

During the CC evaluation of LSD version 6.0, an upgrade release (version 7.0) was being planned. The product development team and I had numerous discussions about possibly switching the CC evaluation to the newer version. There was a chance that by the time we completed the version 6.0 evaluation, version 7.0 would be available and render the version 6.0 certification useless. Since we were approaching the test evaluation phase, changing to version 7.0 would have meant that the developers and technical writer would have to update the evidence documentation starting with the ST up through to the design documentation. Then the evaluators would have to re-evaluate all of the updated evidence. This effort would have set us back several weeks, if not months. We decided that the version 7.0 release plans were too uncertain to warrant changing our evaluation plans and we continued with version 6.0. LSD 6.0 was awarded its certificate in August 2006. LiveState Delivery 7.0 never materialized as the product was obsoleted in 2007.

Reuse Certification Materials

By completing 5 CC evaluations, the SEF team had ample evidence available to reuse from previous evaluations. For those product development teams that are experiencing CC evaluation for the first time, there probably won't be much evaluated evidence available to reuse. Many of the product development teams I worked with were first-timers; nonetheless, I was able to identify evaluated evidence that I could reuse from one evaluation to the next across product teams in different business units.

Symantec software products all went through the same product duplication and delivery processes no matter from which business unit they came. This was true even for newly-acquired companies. It seemed that one of the first things newly-acquired companies did was to adopt the corporate standard product duplication and delivery processes and systems. Since all business units used the same processes and systems to deliver products to the customers around the world, we needed to develop the CC *Delivery* evidence (ALC_DEL) documents just once. The effort we went through to gather all of the information we needed from the various internal departments (order processing, product management, program management, IT and QA) and from third-parties (disk duplication and distribution) was significant. Once we gathered the information, we had to integrate it to make sure that all of the pieces fit together. We also had to account for all of the different ways in which our products could be delivered to our customers: some order appliances (hardware and software bundles), others order media in the form of

CD's and DVD's, and still others have the product delivered over the Internet for download. To put all of this information together was no small feat. However, once we produced the delivery evidence and had it evaluated, we could reuse it for many other CC evaluations. Over time, we did have to make minor revisions as the processes changed, but we did not have to go through the major effort we did for the initial document. This points out to me one of the advantages of company-wide standard processes.

Weekly Status Calls With Evaluators

All good project managers know that the key to managing projects and keeping them on track is to keep the lines of communications open and direct. Every one of the CC evaluation projects I managed held weekly status calls with the evaluators. The conference calls included the key stakeholders – the program manager, a development lead engineer or engineering manager, the CC consultant or technical writer, the evaluators and other people on an "as needed" basis. If there were specific topics or issues that needed to be addressed, we would, for example, invite someone from QA (for test issues) or product management (for marketing questions). The main purpose of the weekly status calls was to make sure everyone knew what the current status of the deliverables were and what to do to prepare for the next steps. If there were any issues that came up or were looming, we would discuss contingency plans.

We held these weekly meetings sometimes even if there was no change in status from the week before and progress was moving along as planned. It was important to make sure everyone got into the habit of reporting status every week. Once-a-week meetings enabled us to make progress on action items and deliverables, but the intervals weren't so long that issues could grow into major problems. Towards the end of the evaluation process and certainly into the validation phase (where we basically waited around for the Scheme to provide us with the certificate), we would meet every two weeks simply because there were few, if any, deliverables for the team to work on.

Weekly status calls with evaluators is a simple practice to put in place and a good habit to establish from the beginning. This helps keep the lines of communication open and reduces delays in responding to questions or issues. It also helps to establish an effective working relationship with the evaluators.

Dedicated Technical Writer

We have discussed the importance of allocating adequate time for the development team to devote to the CC evaluation project. Developers and QA team members must be available to research and provide the technical details about the product and the development process in order to generate the CC evidence. This allocation of time is a sign of the commitment the team is willing to make to the CC evaluation effort. Equally important is the assignment of a dedicated technical writer. The responsibility of this writer is to transform the raw technical details from the development and QA team members into CC evidence documentation that the evaluators can easily consume.

This technical writer can be a contracted, third-party CC consultant. This writer may also be a member of the company technical writing staff. Vendors use different approaches to accomplish this task. During my tenure as Symantec's product certifications director, we used a number of different models. One approach we used worked out quite well for our situation.

The SEF team had hired Jason Traeger as a contract technical writer to develop user manuals for several releases of the product. During his contracted time, Jason learned the product features and company standards for document preparation. The CC evaluation efforts were beginning to ramp up so developing evidence documents became Jason's full-time, permanent job and enabled him to respond quickly to inquiries from the evaluation lab. This responsiveness helped us reduce the overall time it took to complete the evaluation process.

Synchronize Evaluation with Development

Many times the CC evaluation requirement comes up in a *Request for Proposal* (RFP) or *Request for Quote* (RFQ) stage of the procurement cycle. Some customers will not let you be considered for the next step in the cycle unless your product has a CC certificate, is formally *In Evaluation* status, is under contract with a CC testing lab (CCTL) for evaluation, or you have a letter of intent. To address the immediate need for the sales representative to continue to the next step, you must understand what the customer needs by when. If what the customer needs immediately is just a letter of intent - that is easy. If s/he needs a CC certificate immediately, that is impossible if you haven't even started yet.

My model for approaching CC evaluations is that the evaluations should be synchronized in time with the product development process. I believe that you can begin a CC evaluation too early or too late in the product development cycle. Figure 13 illustrates how the evaluation process should start soon after the development cycle begins in order to minimize the time between product release and validation.

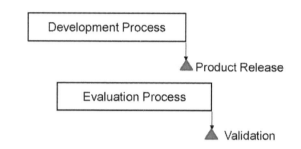

Figure 13: Minimize Time Between Release and Validation

Ideally, you would like to coordinate the development of the CC evidence documentation with the product development phase that would naturally generate the necessary technical content. For example, security architecture and design evidence should be produced during the product design phase. The use of Agile development methods may make evidence creation a bit more difficult, but the development organization must reconcile this as the CC evaluation process tends to assume a waterfall development model.

A CC evaluation can start too early when you engage an evaluation lab before the CC evidence is ready to be evaluated. If certain product design decisions haven't been finalized yet, it would be a waste of time (and money) for the evaluation lab to review and evaluate any preliminary design documents. If the evaluation lab did evaluate and comment on incomplete or preliminary design documents, you would have to pay them again to evaluate the final documents. I have been in situations where customers demanded that we begin a CC evaluation too early for the next release development. In that case, the evaluation lab had nothing to evaluate until the technical details had been worked out and documented.

CC evaluations are only valid for the specific version of the product. For example, the SGS product went through several CC evaluations - each for a different version. Customers generally "forgive" or turn a blind eye to minor releases, but certainly the expectation is that major releases will be CC certified.

It is also possible to start a CC evaluation too late. U.S. government customers are instructed to purchase only CC evaluated products and that includes the specific version of the product. This may be an issue of the U.S. government procurement policy, but from a security purist's point of view, if you cannot prove through evaluation that a subsequent version of a product has not violated any of the security claims made during a previous version's CC evaluation, then you cannot assume that the newer version would pass the evaluation criteria. My advice is to try to avoid starting a CC evaluation on a product version that is already shipping to customers – aim to evaluate a future version.

Project Management Fundamentals

The CC evaluation is a challenging project. It involves coordination with third-parties and coordination with several internal teams. The pressure to perform well is heightened by its high-level visibility (mostly because of the costs involved) and sometimes long time span. To help ensure the success of this effort, my recommendation throughout the evaluation process is to adhere to strong project management fundamentals. This means having a project manager responsible for:

- Planning – establish the overall evaluation project plan and make real-time adjustments as needed throughout the process
- Monitoring – continuously monitor progress and identify issues that affect the plan
- Controlling – mitigate issues and update the plan as necessary

Planning

I always worked very closely with the product development team's program manager. The program manager is responsible for managing the time for everyone on the engineering team. Members of the product development team were oftentimes shifted between different projects as priorities and needs changed. The program manager ensured that the right personnel and equipment were made available according to the master plan – developed and maintained by the program manager. One of the best program managers I have worked with is John Roberts. I worked with John on several CC evaluation projects for the Symantec Mail Security (SMS) product line. The success of those projects was largely due to John's ability to develop the plan and secure the commitment from all of the participants.

From the very first CC evaluation for the SMS Model 8300 in 2007, John demonstrated the ability to gain the commitment from the developers and QA team members. As was our custom, our CC consultant and I met John and the development team at an initial meeting to discuss the evaluation process and everyone's roles and responsibilities.

Early on in the project, we developed time estimates for everyone involved. John needed to know how much time each person would need to devote to this effort. He also needed to know when these people needed to devote this time. Armed with that information, he determined if there were conflicts with other activities (e.g. product releases, Beta test phases). John then integrated the time and personnel allocations for the CC evaluation effort into the master plan.

I've mentioned earlier in this book the need to manage or minimize the scope of the evaluation effort. John helped tremendously in helping the CC consultant and me to understand the complexities of the SMS product and processes. We used that information to establish the TOE boundary, define the evaluated platforms, and identify potential issues with the delivery processes. All of this helped establish a solid initial CC evaluation plan.

Monitoring

We hired Ray Potter from Apex Assurance Group as our CC consultant for several evaluations including the Symantec Endpoint Protection (SEP) product. Ray has a good vendor's perspective having led several CC and FIPS 140 efforts for Cisco Systems prior to starting Apex Assurance. He understands the pressures vendors have from new product release efforts and the occasional hot fix patch release. He also understands the importance of setting visible milestones and monitoring progress consistently. Since we relied on Ray to develop and deliver the CC evidence documentation to the evaluation lab, it was critical that we made sure we were all synchronized to the same schedule. During our weekly status calls with Ray, the development team and the evaluators reviewed the progress toward the current set of deliverables, discussed any issues that might delay any deliveries, and developed contingency plans. We also looked ahead at the next set of deliverables and made sure any dependencies were being addressed. I recall a time when we needed to make sure the evaluation lab had an actual product delivered to them (in Canada) using the standard product delivery process. This required some coordination with the product manager and had to be arranged in advance.

Another valuable skill that Ray brought to us was an understanding from the evaluator's perspective. He understood what the evaluators needed to satisfy their *Common Evaluation Methodology* (CEM) requirements. He also recognized that the more easily and clearly they could identify the evidence elements they were looking for, the quicker we could get through the evaluation. This meant developing tables that clearly showed the linkages between documents such as the functional specifications and the ST.

One of my major responsibilities for such a visible product such as SEP was to make sure that our stakeholders understood where we were in the process. Communicating status to the Sales organization was important because their customers would constantly ask when our flagship security product would meet their procurement requirements. The CC evaluation process can be lengthy (a year or more), so it was important for the Sales team and our customers to be aware of this. It was equally important for them to know where in the process we were all along the way. I would give periodic updates to the Sales team on the status for several of our products going through the CC process. I would also issue letters for our customers announcing the completion of major milestones for those products. These open lines of communication helped quell many concerns and inquiries from our customers and illustrated our commitment to completing these evaluations.

Controlling

Controlling the process is the last step in the project manager's cycle. The successful CC evaluation project manager must drive the product team's responsiveness to inquiries from the evaluation lab. The product developers are responsible for providing the technical details about the product and the development processes under evaluation. Delays in responding to the inquiries from CC evaluators can hinder the success of the evaluation project.

Meg Aronson was the program manager for the SCSP product in 2006 when we began the process to get version 5.0.5 evaluated. Even though the product development team was located in Maryland and she worked in California, Meg was effective at controlling the evaluation process by ensuring that product team members fulfilled their responsibilities to the project. She was also instrumental in making sure that dedicated QA resources were allocated to develop the necessary test suites for the test portion of the evaluation.

The focus of the SCSP team was to get a CC certificate. Several key government customers were expecting it. A timely completion of the evaluation was important to retain credibility with the customers and to address competitive concerns. Minimizing rework of the evaluation evidence was important to reduce the overall time to complete the evaluation. The more time we spent on any one piece of evidence, the more time and money we would spend on the evaluation; it became important to efficiently address any issues and questions that came up during the evidence creation and evaluation. At times it became necessary to get the developers in direct contact with the evaluators. This eliminated any "lost in translation" issues.

Managing Customer Expectations

I have found that it is very important to manage customer expectations. Oftentimes, the motivation for a CC evaluation was to be able to vie for a multi-million dollar government deal where the customer required a CC evaluation. Through our government sales representatives, I would learn that one (or more) of our products would be required to submit to CC evaluations in order to be considered for the contract. The customer would many times just say they wanted a *NIAP certification* or an *EAL certification* with no other details. A few customers would demand that our product evaluate against one of the U.S. government-approved PP. Still others would imply that one of our key competitors had an EAL 4 certificate and if we wanted to compete, our product would have to be evaluated at EAL 4 too.

Whatever the stated customer requirements were, it was important to get them to articulate these requirements as clearly and precisely as possible. Getting details from the customer helps focus the evaluation, reduces cost and saves time.

Once the decision has been made to go forward with the CC evaluation, it is advantageous to communicate this to the customer. I have found that customers at least initially want to see that you are serious about meeting their requirements. Many times, they are only trying to meet the procurement regulations (e.g. NSTISSP #11 or DODI 8500.2) and just need to know that you are moving forward. I have written several letters to customers indicating our plans to engage CC evaluation labs and proceed with the evaluation process being very careful not to be too specific about timelines. I have found it helpful to communicate the intent and plan to move forward to the rest of the government sales team so that they can more readily address other customer inquiries for other contracts.

The Importance of Due Diligence

As the sponsor for the evaluation, you will be paying for the evaluation effort. As the product vendor, you will provide the technical information necessary to create the evidence documentation. You will need to select an evaluation lab and may elect to hire an outside CC consultant to create the evidence documentation. You will be paying the bills and will be responsible for ensuring that you are spending your money wisely.

As with any third-party selection process, you must exercise sound due diligence practices. This means doing some research and setting meaningful selection criteria. In Chapter 8: Partner Selection, I've discussed in detail the factors I think are most important in the due diligence process.

In my experience, I have contracted with labs from 3 different national Schemes and I have used internal and external CC consultants to develop evidence documents. Of the external CC consultants, I have employed consultants who came from the evaluation labs as well as independent consultants. After much trial-and-error, I found the combination that worked most effectively and efficiently for us was when both the evaluation lab and the CC consultant were technically competent and were experienced in CC; moreover, they each respected the other party. This established a level of trust between them. The CC consultant was able to create evidence documentation that was easy for the evaluators to review and meet their requirements in accordance with the CEM. The evaluators appreciated having someone make life easier for them.

This relationship didn't happen by accident; however, it did take some experimenting with different projects to find a real winning combination. I also purposely sought out consultants and evaluation labs that understood our objectives rather than foisting their agenda upon us. Our goal was to successfully complete the CC evaluation as quickly as possible. Having consultants and evaluators that understood that helped us work as a team toward that single goal.

Due diligence plays a role in finding the winning combination for you by learning more about the background and motivations of the parties you are about to hire. The more you know about their experience

191

and knowledge the better your assessment of their ability to help you meet your goals will be.

A Quick Evaluation

Perhaps not surprisingly, the CC evaluation project that completed in the shortest amount of time was one of the last ones I was involved in. Recall that our objective in CC evaluations was to successfully complete the evaluation and receive the certificate as quickly and inexpensively as possible.

Milestone	Date
Contracts signed	December 2006
Draft ST delivered to evaluation lab	January 2007
"In Evaluation"	January 2007
CM/Delivery documents	January 2007
Site visit	February 2007
Design documents	March 2007
Test phase begins	May 2007
Vulnerability analysis documents	June 2007
Certificate award	September 2007

Table 22: Evaluation Timeline

As illustrated in the timeline in Table 22, from start to finish, the EAL 2 evaluation took nearly 10 months. The reasons we were able to complete the evaluation in such a short time was because we followed many of the best practices I've mentioned throughout this book including:

- Sought out and employed competent partners with whom we had good working relationships
- Gained solid commitments from the product development team
- Applied solid project management fundamentals
- Reused evaluation materials
- Carefully managed the scope of the evaluation

Chapter 15: Pitfalls and Pratfalls

As I mentioned earlier in this book, I learned much of what I know about the Common Criteria (CC) from "trial-and-error" – lots of errors. I have experienced many costly, time-consuming and embarrassing mistakes over the years while managing many CC evaluation projects. Some of these mistakes were expected – "let's see what happens if we try this" type situations. Other mistakes were because of poor planning or poor execution. In this chapter, I will relate some of the problems I have encountered in hopes that you will be able to recognize them in your own situations and avoid too much damage from them.

Beware of Protection Profiles

Even though *Protection Profiles* (PP) are developed through a process involving a number of technical experts and a number of review cycles, they can be less than perfect. That is, you may find that there are inconsistencies or errors in the PP. You may find that the specific SFR the authors chose doesn't fit your product's capabilities and you may have to contact the PP authors to try to get a revision to or interpretation of the PP to address issues. In some cases, the PP authors may find that the way your product is designed or implemented is "not secure enough" to meet the security objectives of the PP. At this point, you will have to find an alternative to evaluating against the PP.

In 2002, Symantec acquired Recourse Technologies and I inherited a CC evaluation project that was already underway. The product under evaluation was a network intrusion detection (IDS) product. This project was full of problems partly due to the fact that the product was being evaluated against one of the U.S. government-approved IDS PP. My predecessors committed to pursue this evaluation assuming the product had all of the necessary features to meet the PP SFR requirements - it did not. The eventual result was a completed evaluation, but it cost more and took longer than anticipated.

The IDS PP included the security functional requirement FIA_AFL.1, *Authentication Failure Handling,* that required that the TOE be able to detect when a user-settable, non-zero limit of unsuccessful authentication attempts occurred.

The idea behind this requirement is that if an attacker is trying a brute force attack by guessing the user name and password to log into the system, the *TOE security function* (TSF) would lock the attacker out after a set number of failed attempts. This is a commonly used mechanism – one I'm sure most people have encountered with many everyday IT applications.

There are alternative mechanisms for handling brute force attacks. One used by our IDS system was to increase the time delay between when the user may try again after a failed authentication attempt. That is, after the first failed login, the delay before s/he can try again is 1 second. After the second failed attempt, the delay is 3 seconds. After the third failed attempt, the delay is 5 seconds. The delays grow longer and longer; however, there was no limit to the number of attempts the user can make - s/he just has to wait longer and longer each time. You can argue about whether our method was more secure than the method outlined in FIA_AFL.1. You can also argue that the IDS PP requirement was "implementation- or technology-specific", but as far as the CC evaluator was concerned, our product did not meet the requirement and failed the evaluation.

Modifying our IDS product to use an authentication mechanism as described in FIA_AFL.1 would have been a significant engineering undertaking, so we had to abandon our plans to evaluate against the IDS PP. Your decision to pursue a CC evaluation against a PP should not be taken lightly. You should carefully examine the PP requirements and compare them against your product capabilities.

The Recourse product evaluation was not the last time I would encounter issues with an IDS PP. In 2004, I was surprisingly asked to participate in the development of a new series of IDS PP for the U.S. government. I say "surprised" because up until then I had never heard of any vendor involvement in the development of PPs. This new set of PPs was to be for what they called *medium robustness environments* (MRE). MREs are defined as environments where the likelihood of attempted compromise is "medium" or something more than "basic."

I recall attending a meeting with individuals, all of whom were civilians contracted by the government to develop the PPs. We were reviewing the SFRs that they were proposing to include in the new PP. One of the requirements stated that no alerts should be "scrolled off" the screen until they were acknowledged by the administrator. Apparently these people had never used a network IDS system before - network IDS systems are notorious for generating hundreds or thousands of alerts per hour. Expecting an administrator to acknowledge each alert is not practical. They were also not aware that modern computer systems do not always "scroll" information over a screen. For example, our system would pop up a window if it needed to alert the administrator. These are examples of how PPs can end up with "bad" requirements because they just don't match reality or don't match the features in your product. The lesson to be learned here is that you should take the opportunity to influence the development of PPs.

Incompetent Consultants

All CC evaluation labs must be accredited by their national Scheme, but it is apparent that there is no accreditation process for CC consultants. In my opinion, there are far fewer "problem" labs than there are "problem" consultants.

It is important to do the "buy-versus-build" analysis before you decide to either create your own CC evidence or hire an outside consultant to do the job. Developing CC evidence quickly and efficiently is a coveted skill. It requires the in-depth knowledge of the CC standards, including the *Common Evaluation Methodology* (CEM); the ability to quickly come up-to-speed on the product technology and architecture; and the ability to establish a collaborative relationship with the evaluation lab. A really skilled CC consultant is able to present the technical evidence in a form and format that is easily consumed by the evaluator. That is, the consultant makes it easy for the evaluator to do their job which reduces time and rework – thus saving you money.

Perhaps the most incompetent CC consultant we employed was a contracted technical writer who was learning CC while he was creating the evidence documents. This was his first CC evaluation. He was reading the standards and trying to interpret what was required. We quickly found out that while you can read the CC standards (and even CEM), you still will not be able to capture the nuances and specific definitions of terms unless you have been exposed to CC for a while. For example, in the CEM the evaluator activity for the assurance requirement ADV_FSP.1, *Evaluation of the Functional Specifications*, states that the evaluator will "examine" the functional specification evidence.

If you haven't worked with CC evaluators before, you would only be guessing at what "examine" really means. What will satisfy the evaluator? We found out that no matter how we defined these terms, the evaluator determined what it really meant.

Whether you hire an outside consultant or decide to write the evidence documentation yourself, be aware that even though the CC standards exist, there is a lot of history and assumptions hidden behind them. Learning what all of these hidden assumptions are while you are in the middle of an evaluation can be a very expensive lesson.

Lack of Commitment

Perhaps the biggest reason CC evaluations fail is due to lack of commitment. CC evaluations can take a long time. They certainly cost a lot of money. If they are not properly planned in advance, they can be interrupted by product releases, hot fixes and other higher priority tasks. All of these factors test the commitment of the organization to complete the CC evaluation. Earlier, I discussed the need to develop a strong business case and to identify an executive sponsor or champion; these are to help cement the commitment of the development team during the entire process.

In 2004, Symantec acquired TurnTide. TurnTide had an anti-spam appliance product which had a unique way of filtering email spam. It could filter out spam at the network boundary – before it reached the customer's mail server thus significantly reducing the load on that server. The U.S. government liked this product and had several installations. In 2007, those government customers began enforcing the requirement that IT products be CC evaluated, so we began the evaluation process.

After several false starts, we finally arranged a face-to-face meeting between the CC consultant and the product development team. When we arrived at the Pennsylvania development site, it was apparent that this team was not going to last long. There were many empty cubicles and for some reason, the place was dark. The meeting itself seemed to go well, but I recall feeling we would be pressed to get their full attention on this project in spite of their promises. We continued the project for several months as the team continued to be unresponsive to requests – apparently too busy dealing with higher priority issues.

By the end of 2007, we canceled the CC evaluation project after convincing the product manager that we were wasting everyone's time.

Being CC Ignorant

I live in Silicon Valley, California, U.S.A. I have worked through the "dot.com bubble" and "dot.com bust." I have seen dozens of start-ups appear with nothing but a moderately interesting Internet-based product concept and a pile of money. The notion of "ready-fire-aim" was the way of life here for a long time. Having an idea and just "going for it" was normal. It was more important to be moving forward than to know where you were going. This is not the way to go into a CC evaluation. There is absolutely no excuse for entering into a CC evaluation without first doing your homework and knowing what you are getting into. If you are not well-prepared and don't clearly understand what you need to do, you will fail and end up wasting a lot of time and money.

I talk to a lot of vendors who are learning about CC for the first time. They get a customer requirement that says their product must undergo a CC evaluation. Their sales representatives or executives promise the customer that this will be done so they can close the deal; then the product development team has to determine what they need to do to get this "CC thing" done. Many start by contracting an evaluation lab and then finding out that the development team has to play a more active role in this than your run-of-the-mill IT magazine bake-off test.

In Chapter 4: Do Your Homework, I discussed the need to do some research on the CC standards - get training from experienced professionals, clearly understand your customer requirements, and know your product and development processes. I have been involved in several CC evaluation projects where the product development team did not do some of these steps and paid the price.

Sygate Technologies had a strong suite of network security products including network access control, endpoint protection and on-demand protection. Prior to Symantec's acquisition of Sygate, the U.S. government purchased these products with the expectation that they would be submitted to CC evaluation in accordance with the government's procurement policies. The Sygate team had already contracted with a CC evaluation lab by the time I became involved. In discussions with the evaluation lab manager, he revealed to me that the product development team had failed to deliver a satisfactory *Security Target* (ST) document after several months of engagement. The ST is the first and most important document of the entire evaluation. The ST is the foundation for the evaluation. It defines what will be evaluated; it defines what requirements will be met - without it, the evaluation cannot proceed.

While part of the reason the Sygate evaluation was stalled was because of a lack of commitment from the product team, the major reason for the delay was that they really had no idea what they were doing. They had failed to do their homework before committing to pursue this evaluation. The person who was responsible for developing the evidence documentation thought he understood the product well enough to document it for the CC evaluation; however, he did not understand the CC evaluation requirements and floundered as he tried to understand what the evaluators were looking for.

The product developers and engineering managers were not aware of their responsibilities and the amount of time they would need to devote to this effort. Since their CC evaluation involvement was seen as "unplanned", low-priority work, they did not respond to requests to provide technical information about the product. Also, since Sygate was a new acquisition, the entire organization was subjected to several major process changes – a different product delivery mechanism, a different order processing system, and even a new source code control system. All of these changes not only took time away from the development team, it made it difficult to document the development processes for the CC evaluation. No one was quite sure how things were supposed to work since they had not had the opportunity to experience them yet.

After many months of trying to recover from the poor initial start, we abandoned the evaluation effort for this product. The lesson we learned from this experience is to "look before we leap" into a CC evaluation commitment.

Biting Off More than You Can Chew

If you really have no experience with the CC evaluation process and don't understand the level of commitment required, it may be easy to over-commit yourself or as we Americans say "biting off more than you can chew." Many people hear that CC evaluations are just another product test done by a third-party. There are numerous product tests out there - *PC Magazine* and others frequently acquire products to run tests against them in a "bake off" so that they can publish the comparative results. Most of the time, these tests require little or no interaction with the product vendor and certainly no requirements for the product development team to do anything. If you go into a CC evaluation with that expectation, you will be greatly disappointed.

Symantec's first CC evaluation was with the Symantec Enterprise Firewall (SEF) 7.0 product. The U.K. government, in particular, required that this product be CC evaluated. At the time, many other competitors' products were also pursuing this since the firewall may be the cornerstone security product of any IT organization. Since the firewall is seen as such a critical piece of security technology, customers expect that the evaluations of such products be done as carefully and thoroughly as possible. Many vendors responded by pursing CC evaluations at *Evaluation Assurance Level* 4 (EAL 4) and meeting the requirements of one of the government-approved firewall *Protection Profiles* (PP).

EAL 4 is the maximum assurance level that is internationally recognized. That is, you may have your product evaluated up to EAL 4 in any CC certificate-issuing country and as a result, any other participating country will recognize the certification. This eliminates the need for the vendor to send his/her product to multiple countries for evaluation. EAL 4 is designed to give customers greater "assurance" that the evaluation was performed with greater rigor that EAL 3 or EAL 2. This means the developers must produce more detailed documentation. It also means the evaluator must spend more time scrutinizing the documentation.

The U.S. government published two firewall PPs in the late 1990s – one for *traffic-filter firewalls* and one for *application-level firewalls*. These PPs contained some very specific *security functional requirements* (SFR). These SFRs were designed to reflect the customer's expectations of what security features should be included in a firewall product. These security features centered on how the firewall would protect itself as well as how it would protect the customer's IT network environment.

To try to gain parity with their competitors, the SEF product development team decided their first CC evaluation would be at EAL 4 against the requirements set in the *application-level firewall* PP. They would have to rely heavily on the guidance from the third-party CC consultants they hired. While the guidance they received from the CC consultants was sound, the product development team was nearly overwhelmed with the amount of effort required to meet the requirements. Not only did they have to develop extensive detailed product and process evidence, they also had to change some processes to meet the requirements of EAL 4. I recall that the development facilities had to be upgraded to incorporate electronic identification card readers so they could better control access to the site. They also had to implement, enforce and document a formal visitor access policy.

In the end, SEF 7.0 completed its EAL 4 evaluation but taking much longer and costing much more than originally anticipated.

Poor Lab Relations

It is my belief that if you can establish good personal relations with the individuals with whom you interact, you can accomplish near-miracles. Conversely, if you have really poor relations with those people, you risk failure. I have experienced CC evaluations where the relationships with the CC evaluation lab were excellent and the outcomes were smooth, quick and (relatively) painless. I have also had evaluations where we had poor relationships with the lab and these were arduous, painful experiences.

Obviously, the CC evaluation lab is at the center of the evaluation effort. They are the ones who have to take in the evidence and compare it against the standards. They make the judgment as to whether the requirements have been met or not. They use their experience, skills and biases to make those decisions. They are also under scrutiny by the validators who are charged with ensuring consistency across the labs. Getting them to be on "your side" is an advantage. Having them oppose you will doom the evaluation effort.

Indeed CC evaluation labs should not be unfair to you – after all, you are paying for their services. However, they are also there to uphold the standards and some of them feel an obligation to help improve the security of products. There will invariably be differences of opinion during the course of the evaluation between you and the lab. How you and the evaluation lab handle those situations will determine the kind of relationship you have and ultimately how smoothly the project will proceed.

I have experienced two evaluation projects where the relationship with the evaluation lab was bad – even hostile. The relationship issues in both cases actually were between the CC consultant and the evaluation lab. We all rely upon the person responsible for creating the CC evidence documentation to take the raw technical information and translate it into CC language and CC document format. The idea is to make the raw technical information more easily consumable by the evaluator. It is up to the CC consultant (here I include the internal technical writers we used to create CC evidence as well as the third-party consultants) to meet the CC requirements and expectations of the evaluator.

On one project, our internal technical writer generated some high-level design documents for the *Target of Evaluation* (TOE). The high-level design (required in CC version 2.3) required that the documentation describe the *TOE security function* (TSF) in terms of its major subsystems. It is intended to be a refinement of the functional specifications. At EAL 3, the high-level design also needed to describe the purpose and use of all of the interfaces.

Our technical writer at the time created the design documents to a level of detail and coverage he felt was appropriate; when the documentation was sent to the lab for evaluation, the evaluator disagreed. This disagreement led to a several-week long series of email exchanges, phone calls and meetings. The technical writer was insistent that he was correct. The evaluator (and his manager) felt the evidence lacked the depth of detail required to meet the requirements. The result of this was a significant delay in the project and the eventual release of our contracted technical writer.

Fortunately, I have had many more experiences where the relationship we established with the evaluation lab was much more cooperative and collaborative with much improved results.

In an effort to reduce costs, time and effort, vendors and their customers attempt to "game" the CC system. This form of cheating seems to occur naturally as each party attempts to gain an advantage over the other. In the case of CC evaluations, the battle is between vendors and their customers. The gaming occurs because each party treats CC evaluation as a procurement requirement or "checkbox" item. Both parties are trying to develop a way to get the "checkbox" marked so they can move on with their acquisition and each side seems to equally take part in this game. For every attempt to take advantage of the system, there are counter moves by the other party to try to re-balance the scales. In my experience, I have seen a lot of maneuvering around the U.S. government procurement policies by both the vendors as well as the government customers.

The purpose of this chapter is to make you aware of the games that are being played so that you can be prepared to address them in accordance with your organization's objectives and goals.

NSTISSP #11

The National Security Telecommunications and Information Systems Security Policy number 11 (NSTISSP #11) [NSTISSP] is the national policy governing the acquisition of information assurance (IA) products for the U.S. government. NSTISSP #11 was instituted in 2001 and has been updated over the years. It requires commercial-off-the-shelf (COTS) IA and IA-enabled products to undergo CC evaluations as a condition of procurement by government agencies. U.S. Department of Defense (DOD) directive DODI 8500.2 requires DOD entities to comply with NSTISSP #11. Since the DOD is a big consumer of IA products, there is significant motivation for the vendors to have their products CC evaluated. NSTISSP #11 and DODI 8500.2 are at the heart of much of the maneuvering by COTS product vendors and customers as each try to gain some advantage.

Some government agencies seem to ignore the spirit of NSTISSP #11 by granting their preferred product vendors "waivers" from the requirement to submit products to CC evaluation prior to purchase. Oftentimes, they do this so that they can meet their mission goals and timetables. CC evaluations take months; who can afford to wait that long when national defense systems are at stake? The original NSTISSP #11 included a provision for waivers for products that were acquired prior to the effective dates - often called "grandfathering."

The practice of "grandfathering" products allowed vendors to continue to sell products to the government agencies and departments. If an agency already had a product installed and in use, they continued to purchase the same product under this provision. It seemed you could get away with this charade as long as the vendor didn't change the product's name. Customers seemed to be able to purchase upgrades and additional units without much trouble. Eventually, there were enough violations of the spirit of this directive that an update to NSTISSP #11 was issued in July 2003 so that no "blanket" waivers would be allowed.

Because CC evaluations took so long and could impede an agency's ability to meet its mission goals, the July 2003 update to NSTISSP #11 also stated that if evaluated products were not available, that the agency may require vendors to submit their products for CC evaluation as a condition of purchase. This meant that products did not need to have completed the evaluation and validation process - just to submit the product for evaluation as a condition of purchase. Note there was no stated obligation to complete the evaluation at any designated time. This created a wave of products submitted for evaluation.

Over time, this wave resulted in a pool of products languishing in *In Evaluation* status. Some never completed the evaluation process. Some of those never completed because the vendors didn't know what they were doing and failed out of incompetence and not out of malice. Others however, may have been just gaming the system again to convince their customers to buy the product on the promise that the products would go into CC evaluation.

This game resulted in NIAP issuing policy letter #4 covering "inactive evaluations." That policy letter stated that customers expect a timely completion to products in evaluation.

Policy letter #4 describes the process NIAP developed for dealing with inactive products and removing them from their *In Evaluation* list. Moreover, NIAP also issued policy letter #18 setting specific time limits for evaluations. Evaluations against approved Protection Profiles must be completed within 12 months. EAL 4 evaluations must not take longer than 24 months lest they be removed from the *In Evaluation* list.

The original NSTISSP #11 notice was confusing to government agencies as well as vendors. This confusion prompted Priscilla Guthrie, CIO of the DOD to issue a memorandum [Guthrie] in August 2002 to try to clarify the directive and provide more details on the requirements.

The items this memorandum re-emphasized were related to evaluation against protection profile requirements including:

- If a Protection Profile (PP) for a given product type exists and products have been validated against the PP, then DOD agencies must procure only those validated products
- If a PP for a given product type exists but no products have been validated against the PP, then vendors are required to submit their products for evaluation and validation against the applicable PP in order to be considered for DOD procurement
- If no PP exists for the given product type, then the vendor must submit their products for evaluation and validation against the vendor-provided Security Target (ST)

Protection Profiles (PP) were developed to ensure the government requirements for certain product types were being met. However, in some cases the PPs seemed more like "wish lists" of product features rather than minimum requirements. Some vendors attempted to evaluate against the applicable PPs and many failed. Many more vendors opted to evaluate their products against their own claims covered in their Security Targets (ST) even if a PP existed for their product type – in spite of the Guthrie memo.

With more and more vendors opting to evaluate their products against their own claims and with the drive to reduce the time and costs involved, the scope of the Target of Evaluation (TOE) seemed to shrink. Some TOE scopes shrunk to the point that NIAP felt these evaluations were not serving the government customers. I recall complaints from a former NIAP director that vendors were purposely excluding key security functions from their product evaluations. She mentioned one firewall vendor excluding the remote administration console feature even though this was a normal configuration. I also read an ST for a firewall product which completed a CC evaluation which excluded the ability to block malicious or inappropriate traffic and packet filtering functions as part of the evaluation.

At one point, NIAP issued policy letter #13 (now obsolete) to try to force vendors to evaluate their entire product to prevent them from excluding key features. This requirement was removed as it proved to be impractical to evaluate whole products.

NIAP also issued policy letter #10 requiring that an oversight board review the ST before the product could be officially recognized as *In Evaluation*. The ST review was intended to give the validators an opportunity to make sure the TOE scope was reasonable and sufficient to meet the customer needs for the particular product type.

Another comment I heard from a former NIAP director was that multi-function security products should evaluate against each applicable PP. This would mean, for example, Symantec's Endpoint Protection product that actually includes anti-virus, desktop firewall and intrusion detection (IDS) capabilities should be evaluated against the requirements in the PPs for anti-virus, firewall and IDS. Her assertion was that customers are buying a multi-function product presumably to perform all of these functions; the product should not be allowed to evaluate against just one set of requirements (e.g. only the anti-virus PP). This all makes sense from the customer's point of view – doesn't it? The problem was that each of these PPs were developed independently with different assumptions, so the overlap in the requirements and threats was minimal. It thus was unreasonable to attempt to evaluate against all 3 PPs.

Although Priscilla Guthrie's memorandum to the DOD CIO's was intended to clarify points in NSTISSP #11, one of the paragraphs in the memo caused even more confusion. One of the requirements stated that evaluations must be conducted by a "NIAP-certified" evaluation laboratory.

Based on this comment, government customers began insisting that vendors submit their products for evaluation only to U.S. (i.e. *NIAP-certified*) CC testing labs – in spite of the *Common Criteria Mutual Recognition Agreement* (CCRA). I believe there is an underlying current of distrust by some government customers in evaluations conducted abroad in spite of the CCRA. I have successfully argued with not only customers, but with our own sales representatives that we are entitled to send our products for evaluation at any of the accredited labs from any of the CCRA countries. I've also been able to convince customers by writing letters explaining that NIAP/NSA signed the CCRA.

Another paragraph in the Guthrie memo that caused some confusion seemed to state that vendors could submit products for NIAP (CC) evaluation or NIST FIPS 140-2 validation.

The "or" after the NIAP clause made it appear as though one could submit a product to either CC or FIPS validation - this turned out not to be the case. Vendors that had FIPS validated products thought they were exempt from the CC requirement, but the two requirements are actually separate.

Medium Robustness

For several years, NIAP and the DOD tried to enforce evaluations against so-called *Medium Robustness Environment Protection Profiles* (MRPP). *Medium robustness environments* are basically deployment environments where the threats of attack and potential compromise are higher than your common IT environment. This environment could be in a war zone or around servers containing sensitive information. At any rate, these MRPPs were developed to define the security requirements for products used in those higher threat areas; thus, the PP requirements were more stringent than the basic PPs. The major problem with the MRPPs was the fact that they required something more than EAL 4. That is, the assurance requirements were greater than those that were internationally mutually recognized and so the evaluations had to be performed at a U.S.-based CC lab and the results were not necessarily recognized by other nations. They also encouraged other countries to develop their own country-specific requirements. These unique requirements erode the value of the international standard and force vendors to choose which countries' requirements to meet. Fortunately, NIAP is reworking all of the PPs and the MRPPs appear to be on their way out.

Security Grade

Perhaps the most onerous game we all play is positioning the *Evaluation Assurance Level* (EAL) as the security "grade" of the product. Competitors and customers boldly assert that, "EAL 4 is better than EAL 3" or, "EAL 3 is more secure than EAL 2." I had one customer demand that we evaluate our product at EAL 4 simply because a competing product already had EAL 4 certification – not because the customer needed that level of evaluation. The EAL merely defines the requirements for evaluation – how detailed and in-depth the examination will be, not how many security functions the product has or how secure the product is. People seem to want a simple metric or "grade" to hang on products. They want an easy way to compare "apples to apples." Since CC doesn't provide such a simple metric, customers and competitors use the one number that is easy to pick out of a CC evaluation. I don't think the desire for a simple metric will go away even though product security is a complex, multi-faceted concept. This is an area worth researching.

International Games

Internationally (perhaps more out of ignorance, naiveté or just trying to emulate the U.S. rather than malicious intent), some foreign governments have positioned CC evaluation requirements as barriers to trade. Some countries use CC to take advantage of the fact that it is an internationally-recognized security standard. However, they appear to set up conditions that make it difficult for companies from foreign countries to meet their CC requirements and sell their products in their countries.

The Republic of (South) Korea joined the Common Criteria mutual recognition community in 2007. The Korean IT Security Evaluation and Certification Scheme (KECS) within the National Intelligence Service (NIS) serve as their national CC Scheme. Soon after Korea joined the CCRA, I began to receive inquiries from the public sector sales team in Seoul. Their government customers were advising them that our security products would have to undergo CC evaluations. Normally, this is not an unusual requirement as the focus of many CC evaluations was on security products. Since Korea represents an important, emerging market it was important to try to accommodate their needs.

At first, the requirements went well beyond "normal" CC requirements including providing access to product source code for inspection by KECS. After much debate at various levels in government, KECS developed a set of PPs to capture their requirements that were more in line with the internationally-accepted CC norms. The issue (from U.S.-based companies' point of view) was that KECS was requiring CC evaluations against their own PPs in Korean CC labs only. Not only that, they would require that the CC evidence documentation be in the Korean language. These requirements represented a significant barrier to doing business with the Korean government. If you take the Korean government's point of view, they felt they had unique security requirements and wanted to make sure their needs were being met. KECS had limited resources and dealing with CC evidence documents in the English language posed a problem for them. However, the end result was that this gave an advantage to Korean-based vendors.

The Korean PPs were different from similar PPs developed by the U.S. government. For example, the U.S. has a PP for anti-virus products. Korea developed a PP for anti-virus that had requirements that were different enough that we were potentially faced with having to do two evaluations for the same product – one to meet the U.S. requirements and another to meet the Korean requirements. Again, the PPs were developed with the best of intentions, but the result forced us to carefully examine our business decisions.

Source Code

Source code access is an extremely touchy subject. Product vendors do not want to disclose their software source code because it contains the intellectual property that enables them to hold a competitive advantage over other vendors. From a security point of view, the source code also could reveal weaknesses in the product that if exploited, could place customers' systems at risk. It also seems that some nations simply do not trust other nations (including some of their own allies). This places multi-national product vendors in a tough situation when one government demands access to source code as a condition of purchase while other governments would not buy your product if they knew some other government had inspected your code and now knows all of its weaknesses and faults. I'm sure the U.S. National Security Agency would not want to use a firewall product if they knew another nation had already inspected the code to find out how to hack it.

Under certain circumstances during a CC evaluation (EAL 4 and above), some source code will be revealed to the CC evaluators as part of their examination. During that evaluation, vulnerabilities might be discovered. Some of those vulnerabilities might be reported back to the vendor so that they can be fixed, others may not be reported. This issue is a matter of trust but in the security business you really can't trust anyone. This can however, place the vendor in an uncomfortable situation and will require careful consideration.

Drive Towards Profits

One could argue that many of the tips I've offered in this book (e.g. reduce TOE scope, meet minimum customer requirements, and manage customer expectations) to successfully complete CC evaluations are merely ways to cheat the system and increase corporate revenues and profits. By "working the system" vendors could appear as though they are following the regulations but by cutting corners they are fooling customers and giving them a false sense of security. In order to remain viable, commercial corporations must generate revenue and remain profitable; they do this by satisfying their customers in a cost-effective, efficient manner. The tips I've provided in this book enable product vendors to meet the CC requirements in a cost-effective manner so that they can fulfill their obligations to their shareholders. All commercial vendors have to strike a balance between the need to meet customer requirements, remain competitive and remain viable (i.e. profitable). Some government officials and security purists would claim that vendors who "cut corners" are cheating the CC system – I maintain that what we are doing are being good corporate citizens.

Evaluation labs are also commercial corporate entities with the same need to increase revenues and profits. Some vendors have accused CC evaluation labs of driving their costs up to increase their profits by unnecessarily rejecting evaluation evidence for trivial excuses. Others have claimed that evaluators rejected evidence based on grammatical or spelling errors in the documents. This forced edits to the documents and re-examination by the evaluators. On a time-and-materials contract basis, this increased the costs of the evaluation. Evaluators argued that this is merely urban legend, but the potential for this behavior exists and reinforces the need for vendors to know how CC evaluations work and to work with trusted third-parties.

Vendors and CC evaluation labs are profit-driven, commercial enterprises. While the above allegations may or may not have occurred, it is something to keep in mind so as to maintain the fairness of the evaluation process and business while maintaining a sufficient level of assurance for the customers.

Chapter 17: Smart Card Industry

I am really an outsider to the smart card industry and how they have used the CC to evaluate and test their products. However, what I see is a success story of collaboration between customers, vendors, testing labs and governments. They have figured out a way to make CC work for them. Not surprisingly, the center of this activity is in Europe where the formation of the European Union (EU), the creation of the Euro standard currency, and many European standards are strong indications that the European community sees collaboration as the key to economic success.

Tyrone Stodart and Françoise Forge presented at the International Common Criteria Conferences (ICCC) in South Korea [Stodart 2008] and Norway [Forge 2009] respectively about the history and progress of the Smart Card Industry's use of the CC evaluation methodology. Much of the information I will present in this chapter came from their presentations.

Eurosmart

Eurosmart [Eurosmart] is an international non-profit organization that calls itself the "voice of the smart security industry." Primarily composed of manufacturers, members also include individuals from government, academia, and other industry experts. From its website, they describe their goals as:

- Promoting the image of high security around Smart Secure Devices
- Defending the reputation of the Smart Security Industry
- Promoting Smart Secure Devices and Smart Secure Devices systems standards world-wide
- Building common specifications for applications
- Defining quality test standards

Eurosmart has been instrumental in promoting the use of CC to evaluate smart secure devices. They have also been quite active in the development of applicable Protection Profiles (PP). As of April 2010, there have been 389 CC evaluations of smart devices, many of which were evaluated against PPs.

Eurosmart created the International Security Certification Initiative (ISCI) to manage the technical aspects of standards including certification and tools.

Further, ISCI engages all of the stakeholders with the goal to develop high-quality evaluation standards and to reduce evaluation time and cost. Within ISCI there are two working groups:

1. WG1 - methodology
2. WG2 (JHAS) - technical issues (attack potential and vulnerabilities)

Composition

The Smart Card Industry has a unique evaluation issue - the products they sell are "composed" of integrated circuits (IC), operating systems and "personalized" application software. Examples of these types of products are health identification cards and electronic passports. The CC standards did not easily support the security evaluation requirements for these types of devices.

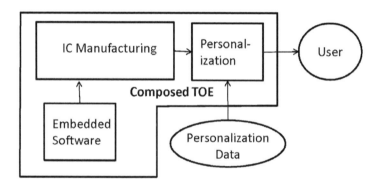

Figure 14: Smart Card Development Process

Figure 14 illustrates the smart card development process where the IC hardware has its own development process and then operating system and application software are loaded and personalized for the end user. To begin to address the needs of these "composed" products, ISCI developed the *Composed Assurance Packages* (CAP). There are 3 different level CAPs where:

- CAP A is structurally composed
- CAP B is methodically composed
- CAP C is methodically composed, tested and reviewed.

As you can imagine, CAP A requirements are the least stringent, then CAP B and then CAP C. CAP adds several assurance families and components to accommodate the evaluation requirements of the composed smart card products. These assurance components deal with the additional interfaces, dependencies and vulnerabilities that arise when product pieces are assembled into a product.

Protection Profiles

Eurosmart and others have developed literally dozens of Protection Profiles (PP) to cover a wide range of smart card products, ICs and modules. Initially, there were two PPs – one from France covering the evaluation of ICs and the other from Germany for systems. This caused some difficulties in composite evaluations because of inconsistencies between the two PPs and a new unifying proposal was developed. A new Security IC Platform PP was developed in 2007 through a collaborative effort between IC manufacturers, composite product vendors, evaluators and certification bodies.

Supporting Documents

In addition to PP development, the Smart Card Industry has developed several *Supporting Documents* (SD) [CC Portal] to provide greater detail to the evaluators on how to consistently conduct evaluations. This effort was necessary even though the evaluation and testing labs had demonstrated that they had the expertise and capabilities to conduct the security tests to a high level of quality. These documents are also updated periodically to keep up with the latest threats and technologies.

- CCDB-2009-03-001: Application of Attack Potential to Smartcards v2.7
- CCDB-2007-09-01: Composite product evaluation for Smartcards and similar devices v1-0
- CCDB-2007-09-02: ETR-template for composition v1.0
- CCDB-2009-03-002: Application of CC to Integrated Circuits v3.0
- CCDB-2010-03-001: Guidance for smartcard evaluation v2.0

Cost and Time Issues

The cost and time requirements for CC evaluations is a concern for the Smart Card Industry as they are for many vendors and they are working on several fronts to address these issues while still maintaining confidence in the security of the evaluated products.

One of the activities the Smart Card Industry has been leading is the concept of "site certification." By certifying a site, evaluators need not spend so much time evaluating site-specific processes that do not change much over time. Site certification is a form of reuse of certification materials that I discussed earlier as a best practice for more experienced vendors.

Manufacturer	# of CC evaluations
Infineon Technologies AG	63
Atmel SmartCard ICs	35
NXP Semiconductors Germany GmbH	35
Philips Semiconductors GmbH	29
STMicroelectronics	25
Samsung Electronics Co., Ltd.	24
T-Systems Enterprise Services GmbH	21
Renesas Technology Corp.	11
Giesecke & Devrient GmbH	10
Sagem Orga GmbH	8
Gemplus SA	7
Sony Corporation	7
ATMEL Secure Products Division	6
Gemalto	6

Table 23: Top Smart Card Companies

Success Story

Table 23 was generated from data gathered from the Common Criteria Portal website [CC Portal] in April 2010. It illustrates that there are a great many smart card vendors engaged in the CC evaluation program. They have also contributed to the development and enhancement of the CC standards through vendor organizations such as Eurosmart to ensure that standards meet their (and their customers') needs.

The graph in Figure 15 shows that not only are smart card vendors engaged in CC evaluations, but evaluation against PP requirements is a big part of their involvement. This result can be explained by the fact that the PPs were developed with significant vendor involvement and required by many of their customers.

The lesson to be learned from the Smart Card Industry is that CC can work for vendors if vendors are actively involved in the community to develop and enhance the standards. This involvement is a reflection of the commitment the Smart Card Industry had made to CC and evaluation. The Smart Card Industry uses the CC effectively to solve some very practical issues to make it a model for others to emulate.

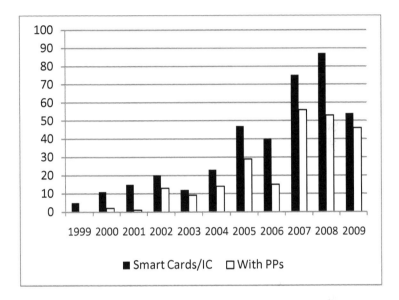

Figure 15: Smart Card Evaluations Summary

PART 5: CONCLUSIONS

In this part:

Chapter 18: Successful Common Criteria Evaluations

Common Criteria evaluations can attract a lot of attention because they are a customer requirement for some governments. They gain visibility because they require a significant commitment of resources. It is a unique type of test that requires deep involvement by the product developers and technical experts. With all of this attention, the goal of any vendor engaged in his/her first CC evaluation is to complete it successfully. But what are the keys to success? The answer to that lies first in understanding what your definition of success is.

What is Success?

Success in any endeavor is defined by your goals. If you achieve your goals - you succeed. Different product vendor organizations may have different goals. The same organization over time may have different goals; the same organization with different products may have different goals for the different products. Each CC evaluation project will be different - starting with its goals.

One goal may be merely to meet a procurement checkbox requirement. The customer said s/he won't buy your product unless you submit it for CC evaluation. You can very easily meet that goal by simply signing a contract with a CC testing lab, write an acceptable Security Target, and get on the *In Evaluation* list. You may not ever complete the actual evaluation, but if the customer "signs the purchase order" and you sales representative closes the deal - you have been successful. This may not follow the spirit or intent of the CC evaluation process or even the customer's procurement policy, but the stated goal has been met.

Another goal may be to retain market parity or gain competitive advantage over a chief competitor that has just completed a CC evaluation at EAL 4. You feel you have to submit your product to CC evaluation as well. You of course, have to evaluate at least at EAL 4 to appear to have the same level of perceived security. Depending on how closely competitive you are with the other company may dictate how committed you are to the evaluation effort. If you are able to complete the evaluation at the level you designated - you have succeeded. Your product may not be any more secure than before but your customer can now recognize that both your product and your competitor's product have undergone the same level of examination.

Every business has personnel, time and money constraints. Every manager is expected to achieve their goals within those constraints. You goals for the CC evaluation may be to complete the evaluation while minimizing the time and cost to complete the evaluation. You may have to meet certain market windows, so timeliness and adherence to schedule would be important. CC evaluations are expensive and large financial commitments are always scrutinized for cost overruns. You can claim success if your CC evaluation completes on time and on budget.

Evaluators, Schemes and some vendors believe CC evaluations can (and should) be used to improve the security of the product and development processes. Using the CC standards to drive product security programs and using the results of CC evaluations to feedback into the improvement process can be their goals. CC standards can provide a language to articulate security requirements. The functional requirements can help define product security features. The functional classes themselves provide a catalog of the families of security functions that can be considered when developing a product. The assurance requirements can be used to define the secure development, delivery, lifecycle and testing processes. For the organization that wants to improve product security, success could be defined as changing products and processes using the CC standards and evaluation results.

Perhaps not as ambitious a goal as changing product features or development processes is to increase awareness of product security issues. Examining CC standards or undergoing CC evaluations may uncover weaknesses in product security features or development processes. This awareness can be an interim goal to actually implementing change and improvement over time.

Earlier in this book, I mentioned that it is possible to start the CC evaluation process too early or too late. If you start the evaluation process too early in the product development process, features and designs may not be complete enough to begin to generate the CC evidence documents. If you start too late in the development process, you may complete your evaluation at the same time (or after) your next product release obsoletes the evaluated version. Your goal may be to maximize the useful life of the CC certificate. That is, you may want to ensure that the evaluation completes as soon after the evaluated version is available to your customers. Success in this case is minimizing the time between product version release and certification.

Some of your customers may have some specific CC evaluation requirements beyond merely "CC evaluation" or "EAL 4." These customers may define some specific security features in the form of a Protection Profile (PP). Your goal may be to meet those specific customer security requirements. In some cases, meeting the functional requirements within a PP may dictate changes to the product functionality. This may mean adding security features that your product did not previously support. It may mean that features will need to be modified to behave the way the customer expects. PPs have assurance requirements as well. If some of your development practices are not up to par with the required assurance level (EAL) requirements, you may be faced with making some process changes as well. You may call your project a success if you can meet all of the functional and assurance requirements in the PP and prove it to the evaluators by completing the CC evaluation.

Whatever your goals, this book was designed to give vendors some tips and guidance on how to be successful in their CC evaluation endeavors.

Keys to Success

This entire book has been dedicated to helping vendors be successful in their CC evaluations. The keys can be summarized as:

- Define clear goals
- Be prepared
- Execute effectively
- Feedback to improve the process

Define Clear Goals

Different CC evaluation projects will have different goals. These goals will depend on your company's strategy and goals relative to product security and meeting customer product evaluation requirements. Your goals will depend on your product's competitive position. These goals may change over time. Set clear goals so that you know if you have been successful when you are done.

Your goals as a vendor will be different from the goals of your evaluator and consultant. They will be different unless you define a common set of goals and you all work toward achieving them together. In my discussions with evaluators, validators and consultants, it is clear they all have different motivations and each have different expectations of the vendor. Some evaluators think all vendors should strive to improve the security of their products and that CC evaluations is the first step toward that goal. Some validators think all vendors products should meet the customer requirements stated in Protection Profiles, so all evaluations should be against PP requirements. Some consultants may want vendors to make more functional claims or evaluate at a higher EAL because the product and processes are capable.

A key to success is defining a set of common goals that you and your partners agree to pursue. This will take a conscious effort on your part to bring all of the parties together to discuss and resolve any differences. Remember, evaluation labs and consultants are commercial entities and driven by their unique business needs. Also, government validators are watching out for their customers' interests and are trying to do what they think will improve the security of the products and systems their governments deploy.

Be Prepared

There are many facets to being properly prepared for CC evaluations. You will need to do considerable background research, investigation, promotion, data gathering and planning. As with any large, complex project, employing solid project management fundamentals will go a long way toward improving your chances for success.

Perhaps the first step in any CC evaluation is to develop a strong business case with supporting arguments for why this project should be funded. Your analysis should include a cost-benefit analysis with a clear and robust return-on-investment. This analysis should provide the quantitative arguments for proceeding with this project. You should also consider the qualitative arguments that will resonate with the thinking and beliefs of the key decision makers. These qualitative arguments could be strategic (e.g. the government business is a key to long-term growth) or competitive (e.g. our key competitors are engaged in CC evaluations) or customer-focused (e.g. product security is expected by our customers). Once you have assembled a strong business case and before you present them to the broader executive team that will make the final decisions and resource allocations, find an executive champion that will shepherd your efforts. You will need him/her to support and defend your project throughout the process.

Knowledge is power. You should know what you are getting into before you commit significant resources to CC evaluations. Do your homework.

You should understand your customer requirements. Some customers are quite definite about what they want – CC evaluation against a specific Protection Profile at a particular EAL with your product running on a select set of operating systems. Other customers will be quite vague – "NIAP certification." Ask your customers questions about what requirements are being placed on them. What regulations must they satisfy? What computing environment are they using? Sometimes the customer doesn't know what they are asking for or what they need. Foresight, experience and knowledge will help you determine the best approach for you and your company.

Before you commit to evaluating your product against a Protection Profile, read the Protection Profile and understand each of the functional requirements. You may need help from a consultant or evaluation lab to help you interpret what the PP requirements actually mean. I have found that what I believed the requirements meant were not what the PP author meant. In order to meet some of these functional requirements, you may have to re-engineer your product or add features. Any changes will take time and will require additional arguments and support to implement them. You may have to make the tough decision of delaying evaluation against a PP to meet a specific customer's requirement in order to just get your first CC evaluation done. This will depend on what your goals are.

Know your product and development processes. We all think we know how our products work, but you may find (as I did) that we don't actually know enough about how our products implement security features. I have also found that no one person really understands the end-to-end product development and delivery process. Development and lifecycle support are major elements of the CC evaluation. Evaluators will be examining an abundant amount of documentation related to secure development practices, secure delivery and secure installation. Vendors typically have either internal or user documentation readily available to address some of the issues the evaluators will be examining but not always everything.

In the process of understanding your product and processes, collect your existing documents. Jane Medefesser, formerly of Sun Microsystems, in her 2007 ICCC presentation "Vendor Strategies for Maximizing Process Under the Common Criteria" [Medefesser 2007] recommends that vendors reuse and recycle evidence documents from previous evaluations. Jane speaks from vast experience and Sun has been involved in CC evaluations for many years, so they have had good opportunities to reuse existing materials. As a first timer, you may have to rely on standard internal documents.

Finally, know your competition and their competitive status with respect to CC evaluations. Have your key competitors completed CC evaluations? What EAL? What versions of the products? Have they been active recently? Basically, do they have a competitive advantage over your products because they have completed or started CC evaluations? Some competitors and some customers think the higher the EAL, the more secure the product is. This is not necessarily true, but you can either try to educate the customer or you can use it to gain a competitive advantage. You can play the "security grade inflation" game by evaluating your product at a higher EAL than your competitor but only if this is consistent with your company's ability and commitment to this effort. I personally don't think this is a good strategy because it propagates the myth that a higher EAL means a product is more secure; it also may be a waste of time.

I have emphasized that managing project scope is particularly important for your first CC evaluation. It is critical not to "bite off more than you can chew." This old saying means don't take on a task that is too big for your organization to sustain and support. I have pointed out that a major way to manage the scope of the CC evaluation is to minimize the Target of Evaluation (TOE) scope. That is, do not include nonessential product features in the TOE. Subsystems or product features that are not "security relevant" or might make the evaluation more difficult or complex should be carefully examined before deciding to include them in the evaluation. At the 2008 ICCC, Masashi Tanaka of the NTT Service Integration Laboratories presented a talk entitled "A smart card evaluation experience under a Japanese Scheme" [Tanaka 2008]. In that presentation, he pointed out that not only did the ELWISE smart card team have to decide on the scope of the TOE, but also the scope of the product lifecycle. The ELWISE smart card is made up of integrated circuits (IC), operating system and application software. The IC's employ a specialized manufacturing and packaging process. They had to consider their business requirements in order to decide the scope of the evaluation.

Identifying and employing competent, cooperative partners can determine the success of your CC evaluation. You can easily find all of the CC evaluation labs associated with every Scheme by searching the Common Criteria Portal website. Each of those labs is accredited by their national Scheme. If you dig hard enough (i.e. read the certification reports) you can see which labs are the most popular. Being popular is an indication of a lab's experience and perhaps their competence, but you should always check references and ask other vendors about their experiences. Finding cooperative labs is perhaps more difficult without some direct experience with them. In a presentation at the 2008 ICCC called "Realizing benefit and value from CC evaluations" [stratsec 2008] stratsec, an evaluation lab in Australia, claimed that through a lab partnership vendor development processes could integrate the evaluation needs resulting in a more efficient evaluation process. This may be true but finding the partner that will work with you and align with you goals takes some effort.

Unlike CC evaluation labs, CC consultants are not accredited. There is no single list of available CC consultants as there are with CC evaluation labs. Finding competent and cooperative consultants takes more effort than finding a competent and cooperative evaluation lab. Relying on other vendors and learning from their experiences with consultants becomes a primary method for vetting consultants. Obviously, checking client references and obtaining background information (e.g. resumes, CVs) about the consultants are critical to assessing the competency of the consultants. The Common Criteria Vendors' Forum (CCVF) [CCVF] has many members who have used consultants and may be willing to share their experiences with others.

Resource allocation and project planning solidifies the commitment of the organization to proceed with the CC evaluation. Your plans must include not only internal development team members, QA and product management, it must also include the tasks and deliverables for the consultant and evaluation lab. This plan must answer the question, "Who does what by when?" There must be sufficient detail in the plan to recognize dependencies and the impact of any delays. The resource allocation plan makes it clear how many resources (people) will be required, when and for how long. This plan, of course, will be reviewed periodically as the project progresses and updates will be made during the execution of the project.

Execute Effectively

Once the initial planning has been completed, it is time to execute the plan. Executing the plan effectively requires the application of the sound project management fundamentals of monitoring and controlling.

CC evaluation project monitoring takes the form of weekly project status meeting (usually conference calls) to assess the status of each participant relative to the project plan, to identify issues that may impact the plan, and to discuss preparations for next steps. If any issues are identified that might cause a schedule slip, contingency plans need to be developed. It is important that the evaluation lab is kept busy doing useful evaluation work at all times. If evidence documentation for one evaluation work unit is held up, then evaluation resources should be shifted to another work unit. That way, even if one work unit has been delayed, the overall schedule does not slip.

A key aspect to controlling the project is ensuring timely responses to inquiries and observations from the evaluation lab. When an evaluator has a question, it is imperative that the consultant and/or the developer respond as quickly as possible. In my experience, a major reason CC evaluations failed is because developers did not respond to questions in a timely manner. Delays in response usually indicate a lack of commitment and lack of commitment dooms the project. On the other hand, timely responses indicate a strong commitment and a good chance for success.

Feedback to Improve the Process

No matter what your business goals are, you should work towards making the next CC evaluation go smoother, faster and cheaper than the last one. If, in order to meet your customer needs you are required to submit your products to CC evaluations, then, as a good corporate citizen you must strive to reduce the cost to complete these evaluations. Learn from your experiences. Learn from others' experiences. Ideally, what you learn will be applied to the next CC evaluation to reduce time, reduce costs, improve response to customer requirements (and thus increase revenues), and improve product and process security understanding (if not improve product and process security).

Oracle Corporation wrote a white paper entitled "Oracle Software Security Assurance Process" [Oracle]. In that paper they point out that formal security evaluations are valuable in demonstrating the security of a software product. The paper goes on to recognize that submitting products to formal, independent evaluations using internationally recognized security standards demonstrates the vendor's commitment to security. Customers expect some level of assurance that the products they purchase from you meet their security expectations –

both in terms of product security features and in terms of secure development processes that reduce the introduction of exploitable vulnerabilities. Success can be measured by the level of customer acceptance of your products to meet their security assurance needs and expectations.

Chapter 19: Issues with the Common Criteria

Perhaps the best documentation of the issues of Common Criteria was assembled by the Technical Standards and Common Criteria Task Force in 2004. This task force was an industry-led coalition of interested security experts from the public and private sectors created as part of the National Cyber Security Summit process. Task force members came from a variety of areas including trade associations; non-profit organizations; publicly traded and privately held companies; and state, local, and federal government employees. The co-chairs were Mary Ann Davidson of the Oracle Corporation, Edward Roback from the National Institute of Standards and Technology (NIST), and Chris Klaus of Internet Security Systems (now IBM).

The task force was formed to identify gaps and develop recommendations to promote the adoption and implementation of the President's National Strategy to Secure Cyberspace. In the area of technical standards, the task force was directed to seek ideas on how to bring together and leverage expertise within the private and public sectors to develop new tools, technologies or practices that can reduce vulnerabilities at every level. In the specific area of Common Criteria (CC), the suggested focus was on developing recommendations to improve the CC evaluation process, as well as to explore alternative mechanisms as it pertained to more effective industry usage and compliance, and enhanced government guidance and support. I chaired and led the working group dedicated to addressing the Common Criteria, NIAP and security metrics. In April 2004, we released the "Technical Standards and Common Criteria Task Force Recommendations Report" [NCSP]. Within that report, the Common Criteria, NIAP Review and Metrics Working Group proposed 35 recommendations in six core focus areas:

1. Increase the NIAP Evaluation Scheme effectiveness
2. Make government commercial off the shelf (COTS) procurement policies realistic
3. Reduce the costs of CC evaluations
4. Increase the demand for CC-evaluated products
5. Improve the use and utility of Protection Profiles (PP)
6. Increase product security through CC specifications and evaluation

In each focus area, the working group discussed the current landscape and provided specific findings and recommendations targeted for both government and private sector action. These recommendations were intended to address the issues with CC and to make it a viable, value-added process towards improving the security of the products within our information infrastructure. The report cited the following advantages of CC:

- Internationally recognized standard
- Designed to describe security requirements of systems and components
- Helps improve security of vendor processes and products
- Standardized certification is an industry cultural catalyst for change

The issues that were discussed in the task force report and still exist with vendors that are dealing with CC today are:

- Reduce the costs of CC evaluations
- Increase the demand for CC-evaluated products
- Improve the use and utility of Protection Profiles (PP)
- Increase product security through CC specifications and evaluation

CC evaluations can cost hundreds of thousands and, in some cases, millions of dollars. These costs are not often offset by incremental sales revenues, so developing convincing business justifications for pursuing these evaluations is difficult. These costs are particularly prohibitive to smaller companies and essentially serve as competitive barriers for them. Some of the recommendations from the task force that addressed this issue included:

- Make greater education available to vendors on how to more effectively navigate through the process and how to maximize evidence reuse
- Examine alternative faster, more nimble evaluation methodologies to speed up the evaluation process
- Develop a mechanism to accommodate minor product changes (e.g. patches) without completely invalidating the certification

Common Criteria certifications may be internationally recognized by 26 countries but they are virtually unknown outside of government circles. Commercial companies do not recognize the value and thus do not require CC evaluations. The lack of demand exacerbates the evaluation cost issue. The task force made the following recommendations to improve this situation:

- Vendors, evaluation labs and Schemes should promote CC more
- Customers should promote an environment of competition on security and assurance
- Country-specific or market segment-specific product evaluations should be discouraged

Protection Profiles (PP) were designed to capture customer security requirements. Competing products evaluated against the same PP enables customers to do an "apples-to-apples" comparison. Some of the following recommendations related to PPs were included in the task force report:

- Consortia of vendors, customers, evaluators and government should develop and vet PPs in an open forum
- Develop a mechanism by which products can be "graded" against multiple PPs as more multi-function products are being developed
- PPs should include evaluation against a standard set of vulnerability tests

Many of the current U.S. government-approved Protection Profiles were developed with insufficient input from end user customers, vendors and evaluation labs. The result has been that very few products have successfully completed evaluation against these PPs. Customers do not require or request evaluations against these PPs partly because they see no relationship between the requirements stated in the PP and their real-world requirements. In some cases, vendors have complained that some of the PPs are merely "wish lists" of product features and not a realistic set of security needs. In some cases, the requirements are so specific as to dictate a particular technology that could stifle the innovation of perhaps more effective, cheaper or more efficient technologies.

The Smart Card Industry seems to have found a formula for engaging customers, vendors, evaluation labs and government to develop useful Protection Profiles and supporting documents that address customer concerns, are practical, and are testable. This may serve as a model for future CC engagements.

Customers expect CC evaluations to improve product security; evaluators and government also seem to expect this. However, CC alone is not designed to accomplish this. Many vendors see CC evaluations as merely procurement "checkboxes" and have little incentive to put more effort into it. The task force recommended:

- Providing more vendor education and training on how to gain greater benefits from CC evaluations
- Experienced vendors should be encouraged to share more of their positive experiences with CC

Little has changed and few of the recommendations that were made were ever completed (or attempted) since 2004. The major issues still remain partly because their solutions are elusive and complex.

Over the years, I have been quoted in several articles criticizing the Common Criteria and highlighting the issues vendors have experienced with it. In a May 7, 2007 Government Computer News (GCN) article called "Common Criteria is bad for you" [Symantec], I pointed out that CC is a static product analysis – that CC evaluations are only valid for a given product version. Given the speed with which (software) product security updates are made today and the long evaluation periods, this puts government systems at risk if all they are only allowed to install are evaluated product versions.

In the June 13, 2007 GCN article "Under Attack: Common Criteria has loads of critics, but is it getting a bum rap?" [Under Attack], Alan Paller of the SANS Institute criticized CC evaluations as a paperwork exercise. Fiona Pattinson of atsec counters that criticism stating that documentation evaluation is a sound way to assess product designs in her 2007 ICCC talk entitled "Common Criteria in the Real World" [Pattinson 2007]. In either case, the time it takes to evaluate products is a concern that should be addressed.

In the May 7 GCN article, I also pointed out that CC does not address coding vulnerabilities – software implementation errors that can be exploited to expose user data or disrupt normal operations. This sentiment is echoed in a blog entry by Eric Bidstrup at Microsoft on December 20, 2007 [Bidstrup] stating that Common Criteria evaluations do not address implementation vulnerabilities such as buffer overflows. This leads to my point that CC is not recognized by commercial customers partly because it does not address one of their chief concerns – code vulnerabilities.

The key issues from a vendor's perspective for Common Criteria can be summarized as:

- Focus on static product assessment
- Long evaluation times relative to product development cycles
- Coding vulnerabilities are not addressed
- Not recognized or required by commercial customers
- CC does not improve product security

Static Product Assessment

By the very nature of product evaluations, the Target of Evaluation (TOE) must remain static during the course of the evaluation. Any changes made to the TOE during or after the evaluation could invalidate the claims made and thus no assessments made by the evaluators can be guaranteed without further examination. Common Criteria evaluations are valid only for the evaluated product version on the assessed platforms and in the designated configurations. This "inflexibility" and static nature of the evaluations runs counter to the fast-paced change of commercial IT product development cycles. To complicate matters further, security patches are issued on a regular basis to mitigate discovered vulnerabilities. Without these patches, customers may be at greater risk using evaluated but unpatched product than an unevaluated but patched product.

Symantec product teams were encouraged to purchase (buy rather than build) cryptographic library modules whenever cryptographic functions were needed within the product. As the director of software assurance, I also encouraged product teams to purchase libraries that had FIPS 140-2 validations so we could meet the U.S. government customers' requirement pressed upon them by the Federal Information Security Management Act (FISMA). Sadly, many of the FIPS 140-2 modules that were available did not support the breadth of platforms our products required. Similarly, our own CC evaluations were limited to a few platforms. We limited the number of evaluated platforms for cost and efficiency reasons, but for some customers this posed a problem as some of the platforms they desired were not the evaluated platforms.

CC assurance (or certificate) maintenance programs are now available to make it easier to update evaluations and certifications. This usually involves some documented justifications for what changed since the last evaluation along with updates to some of the evidence documents. This works fine for minor patches and minor releases. Certainly major releases and major product changes require a full re-evaluation with hopefully some evidence reuse. My point however; is: every version of every product should be evaluated so that our customers have

233

the same level of assurance for every release and every patch for every product.

Long Evaluation Times Relative to Product Development Cycles

CC evaluations can take months or even years depending on the complexity of the product under evaluation as well as a number of other factors. The long evaluation cycles heighten the issue that the evaluations are assessments of "snapshots" in time of the products. Product development cycles are being driven to shorter and shorter intervals in order to meet customer and competitive demands for new features, security updates and defect patches. CC evaluation periods are out of synch with modern product development cycles and this causes vendors to have to think hard before engaging in any evaluation.

Long evaluation times are a disservice to customers. Customers want and need the latest product versions and updates. They have time and competitive pressures themselves. Their missions and goals may be compromised if they cannot obtain products with the necessary features. Today, customers are faced with having to choose a product that is secure (i.e. with the latest security patches applied) or a product that has been evaluated (e.g. an older version). Some government customers are encouraged (if not required) by regulation or policy to purchase and use only CC evaluated products. If vulnerabilities are later discovered in the evaluated version, customers are faced with the decision to patch the product and basically invalidate the certified version, wait until the vendor evaluates the newer version, or continue using the evaluated but potentially riskier version. This should not be a choice the customer should have to make.

Independent, third-parties evaluations naturally take time as the evaluators learn about the product technology, product features and development processes. They must understand the product architecture, product functionality and designs. Evaluators must also learn the details of the vendor's development and delivery processes; then, they can do an assessment against the claims in the Security Target. This "learning curve" time extends the evaluation time especially if this is the first evaluation for the product and the first exposure to this type of technology for the evaluator. Certainly as the evaluators gain more experience through repeated evaluations the learning time is decreased.

In my experience, the biggest source of delays during the CC evaluations is the lack of responsiveness by the developers. Delayed responses coupled with the lack of contingency plans to avoid evaluator "dead time" result in overall longer evaluation cycles. Developers often get pulled away to higher priority issues or projects. If developers cannot respond to questions or issues from the evaluators, then the evaluation process can be stalled. Since higher priority issues are commonplace in today's business world, it is critical that the evaluation project manager exercise strong project management fundamentals to minimize the impact of these disruptions.

Coding Vulnerabilities Are Not Addressed

As Eric Bidstrup of Microsoft noted in his blog of December 20, 2007 entitled "Common Criteria and answering the question 'Is it Safe?'" [Bidstrup], CC evaluations may not do an adequate job of uncovering implementation vulnerabilities. Implementation vulnerabilities are the vulnerabilities introduced in the software that result in things like buffer overflows and cross-site scripting errors. These vulnerabilities can be exploited by viruses and worms to gain unauthorized access to customer data or cause disruption in customer's activities.

Preventing the introduction of implementation vulnerabilities in IT products has grown in importance as the exploitation of these vulnerabilities has led to costly and embarrassing data breaches and service outages. This has become a highly visible concern for customers. There is growing dissatisfaction from customers and government that vendors perhaps are not doing enough to address this problem.

CC evaluations at the lower assurance levels (EAL 1 through 4) do not provide the kind of evidence (i.e. source code) that evaluators would need to do an adequate job of searching for implementation vulnerabilities. In my opinion, I wouldn't want CC evaluators to examine my product's source code for implementation vulnerabilities simply because I do not believe they have the expertise to do so. Vendors hire security consultants who have specialized expertise to do design and code inspections as well as penetration tests for the specific technology involved. Many product vendors employ internal and external security consultants for these tasks. CC evaluations don't give vendors any "credit" for such activities since the search for these types of vulnerabilities do not fall within the scope of CC evaluations even though these activities may address customer concerns.

Not Recognized or Required by Commercial Customers

Although the CC is an international standard (ISO 15408) and certificates are mutually recognized in 26 countries, there is relatively little demand for CC evaluated products. Outside of government and government-controlled or government-regulated entities, very few commercial enterprises recognize CC certifications. Commercial enterprises and (household) consumers represent the vast majority of revenues for most commercial product vendors; that means they drive the direction, strategy and motivations of the commercial product vendors. If these commercial customers demanded CC evaluations, vendors would be elbowing each other out of the way to pursue them. If commercial customers demanded CC evaluations, the vendors would not complain so bitterly about the costs of evaluations. The evaluation costs can be more easily amortized over the broader base of customers; this makes justifying the large investment easier as well.

If more commercial customers demanded CC evaluations, most of the complaints from vendors would wane. Commercial vendors would gladly invest a million dollars in something if they thought they could make $100 million or felt $100 million of existing business was at stake. I've heard arguments from government customers that the government expects to spend billions of dollars in IT security over the next year, so vendors should invest in CC evaluations. That is a lot of money, but the government is not one entity with a single purchase order for CC evaluated products. The government is made up of hundreds of agencies and perhaps thousands of projects - each with their own mission and product requirements. In spite of regulation and policy, each purchase is treated by the customer and the vendor as a single transaction, so in most cases there is little leverage.

Vendors also need to consider lost opportunity (revenue) costs. For every minute and every dollar spent on CC evaluation efforts, commercial product vendors are choosing not to invest that time and money on more competitive product features, better quality, improved performance or better customer service – all things that almost guarantee an increase in incremental revenue. CC evaluation efforts can easily result in no incremental revenue. A vendor can spend hundreds of thousands of dollars and hundreds of person-hours on preparing for and executing a CC product evaluation. There is no guarantee that sales for that product will increase because it is now CC evaluated.

CC needs to do a better job of addressing commercial customer (perceived and real) product security needs. If susceptibility to viruses and worms are a major concern to the mass market, then CC evaluations should provide customers some level of assurance that evaluated products have done something to mitigate or eliminate the possibility that exploitable vulnerabilities exist in that product.

CC Does Not Improve Product Security

Over the years, I've been asked by many people whether or not CC evaluations improved product security. I guess the answer is – it could but doesn't always or it can help but not by itself. I like to compare CC evaluations to weighing myself. If I hop on the scale and it says I weigh 160 pounds, does the scale make me lose weight? No, not by itself. It certainly can help me recognize that I may need to lose weight if I wanted to weigh less than 160 pounds, but the scale and the weight measurement by itself do not take any action to get me to shed those pounds.

Regardless of what the original goals of the CC were in 1999, some customers and evaluators today expect the CC to improve product security. They expect that product vendors will recognize security flaws in their products during the evaluation process and strive to improve their products. They expect that vendors will move beyond treating CC evaluations as a procurement "checkbox" and use it to motivate and direct improvement. This evolution may occur if enough customers demand it of their vendors.

Chapter 20: The Future of the Common Criteria

What will the future hold for the Common Criteria? Will it wither and fade away from neglect as did the *Orange Book* in the 1980s? Will it gain momentum and acceptance from the broader marketplace? The answer will depend on how the leaders of the Common Criteria standards and implementation around the world address the issues presented in the previous chapters – and who those leaders will be. To date, the governments (CC Schemes in particular) have been driving the CC standards and the implementation policies. The Smart Card Industry has shown that this does not have to be the case - the vendor community can play a much bigger role in defining the course of the CC.

CCDB Plans

In 2008, David Martin, chair of the Common Criteria Development Board (CCDB) and the director of the U.K. Scheme [CESG] presented plans for the next major revision (4.0) to the CC standards. He began by emphasizing that the CCDB has heard the criticisms from customers, vendors and Schemes and vowed to address them. Since many of the comments and feedback have been about how CC affects general-purpose software products, the focus has been on addressing issues from that sector. David summarized the needs of the vendor community based on the feedback and comments he has received over the years. The vendor needs he identified were:

- An assurance process that takes account of all of their assurance efforts
- An efficient process (both fast and cost effective)
- A process that helps them further improve
- Results that are valued by end customers
- Results that are widely usable/recognizable as possible

It is clear from these items that the CCDB members have heard the complaints and issues that the commercial software product vendor community has been voicing for several years. These needs reflect the issues we covered in the previous chapter of this book. The vendor complaints that the CC evaluations take too long, cost too much, are not relevant to customer needs, and do not give enough "credit" to vendor product security efforts are all covered by these topics.

While the product vendors attempt to reflect their end customer needs, the CCDB also collected comments directly from end users. Some of their needs were:

- Assess assurance in operation
- Provide meaningful assurance information
- Evaluate real products as they are delivered and used in the marketplace
- Evaluate in a predictable and cost-effective manner
- Enable qualitative product assurance comparisons

These comments illustrate the need to provide more information that is relevant to end user operational security issues. The users want a way to do "apples-to-apples" comparison of product assurance claims. They want to know what assurance they can expect in their real-world deployments. They also are concerned with the timeliness and costs of evaluations.

In response to these concerns, the CCDB launched several working groups to begin the investigation process leading up to proposals and trial solutions. There were 5 working groups led by different Schemes:

1. Evidence-based approaches
2. Skills and interactions
3. Predictive assurance
4. Meaningful reports
5. Tools

The evidence-based approaches working group is led by the U.S. and Swedish Schemes. They are examining how to acknowledge and provide credit for alternative or complementary evaluations and activities that vendors exercise to provide greater assurance. Vendors that engage in other third-party testing programs such as ICSA Labs or Checkmark testing would like to at least not have to reproduce such functional tests and ideally leverage those test results into the CC evaluation. The challenge here may be to determine how these other types of tests fit within the framework of assurance as defined by the CC.

The skills and interactions working group led by the U.K. and U.S. Schemes are examining how to improve evaluator effectiveness and consistency. One of the complaints from vendors has been that evaluation results vary greatly from Scheme to Scheme, lab to lab, and evaluator to evaluator. This working group is considering how additional training, evaluator assessment and increased interaction between evaluators may address this situation.

The predictive assurance working group is led by the German Scheme. The aim of this effort is to address the issue that product development processes don't change much over certain intervals of time, so why should these processes be re-evaluated from one product to the next coming from the same organization? As Jane Medefesser [Medefesser 2007] pointed out in her 2007 presentation, much of the process evidence can be reused from one evaluation to the next primarily because the processes had not changed much. A goal of the predictive assurance working group is to determine how to make statements about the assurance of one product evaluation based on previous evaluations from the same organization by examining the vendor's development and flaw remediation processes.

The meaningful reports working group is chartered to address the user need to gain more useful information about the evaluation. This group led by the Canadian Scheme aims to help users understand the security architecture, residual risks, and the effective use of the security mechanisms in the evaluated products. This may entail modifications to the content and format of the publicly disclosed reports and documents output by the evaluation and certification.

The Spanish Scheme has been working on the topic of tools and techniques for several years now. The goal of this working group is to define workflows and to encourage the use of tools by vendors. This work is aimed at reformulating the requirements in the assurance family ALC_TAT – tools and techniques and augmenting evaluations with supporting documents.

The progress of these working groups has been slow - partly due to resource constraints, but it is encouraging to see that the issues have been recognized and working groups have been established. The original goal was to have CC version 4.0 out by the end of 2010. That goal may not be realistic given the lack of significant progress in the past year or two.

Common Criteria Vendors' Forum

In 2004 and 2005, at my urging, the Cyber Security Industry Alliance (now part of TechAmerica) sponsored two Common Criteria

Users' Forums. These forums were intended to bring the CC industry together to discuss issues and propose solutions. The invited attendees included product vendors, evaluators, validators and a very few government customers. Through these discussions it became clear that the commercial product vendor community had the most issues with the CC and also had a perspective different from the evaluation labs and the government.

In 2004, I co-founded and now still chair the Common Criteria Vendors' Forum (CCVF) [CCVF], an informal collection of representatives from commercial product vendor companies. The members have first-hand experience with the CC evaluation process or are faced with that possibility. There are currently over 120 members on the CCVF mailing list from companies around the world. We gather to discuss Common Criteria and CC-related issues, develop solutions, and drive action to improve CC. We accomplish this by creating awareness of the issues and to provide a single voice as a vendor community to the standards bodies and policy makers. Some of the original objectives of the CCVF are:

- Reduce the time and effort required to complete CC evaluations
- Create useful, realistic Protection Profiles
- Develop a viable strategy to deal with composed systems
- Support a viable certificate renewal process

Commercial product vendors, to date, have had little say in the CC policy and standards development efforts. CC version 3.0 was intended to correct problems in version 2.x, but the commercial product vendors were not part of the standards development process. As a result, fundamental problems such as the fact that CC evaluations are static evaluations of a "snapshot" of a product run counter to the dynamic nature of commercial IT product development remain. Another issue is that because CC evaluations take so long, evaluated products may be obsolete by the time the certification is awarded. CC certifications are not recognized as adding value to many customers, especially non-government customers, because the standards do not focus on security issues that most commercial customers care about. It also fails to recognize the efforts vendors put forward to mitigate and reduce the number of code vulnerabilities in their products.

We encourage commercial product vendors to join the CCVF so that we may include your concerns and issues in our discussions with the standards and policy makers. Your participation will lend greater weight and credibility to the comments and proposals the CCVF makes. Collaboration with CCVF members gives you the opportunity to see diverse approaches to every day CC process challenges. You'll gain insight into new and up-coming standards and policy changes and their impact on product vendors. You will have the opportunity to contribute to developing solutions to problems and issues we all face

It is through greater vendor involvement in the CC development process that we can improve the CC and make it more valuable and useful to our customers. CCVF members are already involved in the CCDB working groups. It is also partly due to the CCVF's "voice of Industry" that the CCDB has heard, and has begun to address the concerns vendors have complained about for years – CC costs too much, takes too long, and doesn't add value.

The CCDB and NIAP have recently been talking about greater use of "communities" to develop and move forward plans to improve CC. One of the goals of the CCVF has been to encourage and gain greater participation in the development of Protection Profiles. NIAP has responded and is much more open to vendor input and participation to their efforts.

I believe that the future of CC should be decided by the community of customers, vendors, evaluators, validators and Schemes coming together to develop strong, robust solutions to the problems and concerns of all stakeholders. The CCVF is one vehicle for vendors to have their issues known.

Protection Profile Development

Throughout this book, I have mentioned the issues I've encountered dealing with Protection Profiles (PP). I have counseled that vendors should be wary before engaging in evaluations against some of the existing PPs. My experience has shown that these PPs have flaws that could cause vendors to go through contortions trying to meet the requirements while the requirements themselves are ill-conceived. I have also seen that some PPs have been developed by people who have insufficient background and experience with the technology. NIAP plans to address vendor concerns by updating the set of existing Protection Profiles. It also seemed to me that there was inadequate input from the end user community to the requirements definition process.

The Smart Card Industry has had end user, vendor and evaluation lab participation in the development of the set of PPs they use to evaluate their products. They have adapted the CC to meet their needs including the creation of the composition assurance package to deal with the fact that smart cards are composed of integrated circuits, operating system software, and application software. They have also developed a set of supporting documents to provide greater detail and specificity to the evaluation requirements. They were able to accomplish all this through the combined and collaborative efforts of all of the major stakeholders. This model may be one which can be adopted for the general-purpose software community to address their issues.

Outside of the smart card industry, the U.S. government has been the largest sponsor and producer of Protection Profiles – mostly for security products such as firewalls, intrusion detection systems, and public key infrastructure (PKI). Recently, NIAP has been requesting more vendor input and participation in the PP development efforts. The working group developing the new firewall PP is led by Laura Stubbs of Cisco Systems and Jane Medefesser of Juniper Networks. Joshua Brickman from Computer Associates (CA) and Booz Allen Hamilton are leading an effort to develop a PP for enterprise security management (ESM), a new class of product. NIAP has begun an effort to replace or update all of the PPs they had developed. This effort attempts to correct the problems with the existing set of PPs and to address some of the broader issues with CC.

By design, anyone or any organization can develop a PP and have it validated. Usually the PP is developed to reflect the needs of a relatively large group of users. Users are given the freedom to define and articulate their security requirements for a specific product type in the form of a PP. Ideally, the requirements in the PP should reflect a large enough population of users that warrant such an effort; however, there is no requirement to coordinate like efforts around the world. The U.S. government developed an anti-virus PP in 2004. The South Korean government developed their own anti-virus PP in 2007. The two PPs are similar but different enough that it would be difficult to do one evaluation to cover the requirements in both PPs. This may result in an anti-virus product vendor having to decide whether to evaluate against the requirements in the Korean PP or to evaluate against the requirements in the U.S. PP. What I call "Protection Profile proliferation" is a real issue because if more organizations or nations decide to create their own PP to meet their own perceived unique security requirements, the major advantage of CC evaporates. The greatest strength and advantage of the CC is that vendors can evaluate their product once under this regime and have that certification recognized around the world. If a vendor has to evaluate and certify his products against different PPs for each country, then the value of CC degrades.

Forming international communities to develop internationally-recognized Protection Profiles will eliminate Protection Profile proliferation. As we develop communities to develop PPs we should make sure that we include members from a wide variety of geographies, market segments and organizations. Developing internationally-recognized PPs augmented perhaps by tools such as supporting documents may mitigate some of the evaluation consistency issues we've experienced in the past.

Software Assurance and Security

Some vendors such as Oracle Corporation [Oracle] have integrated CC evaluations into their secure product development processes. Microsoft [SDLC] and EMC have developed strong secure development lifecycles and product security programs. These companies serve as great examples of how CC evaluations can be used to migrate from just being a procurement "checkbox" to becoming part of a program to improve product security.

The argument about whether CC evaluations help improve product security or help products become "safe" should be addressed. Working together, commercial product vendors, evaluators and government can put together plans and weave those into CC improvements. The current set of working groups led by the CCDB is a start to address these issues. Product vendors can and should take a leadership role in defining how this should work. Given that many product developers have product security programs in place and have defined metrics, best practices, tools and processes, it should be natural that those organizations take the lead.

The Common Criteria provides a solid foundation and framework upon which to build and enhance to address the product security concerns of customers and vendors now and into the future.

Closing Remarks

At the beginning of this chapter I said the future of CC will be determined by where the leaders of the CC take it. The question is: "Who will lead the CC?"

For the most part, governments have funded, supported, developed, enhanced, maintained and led the CC standards and implementation efforts. The Smart Card Industry has illustrated that they can make the CC serve their purposes by creating communities of government, vendors, test labs and customers to develop PPs and supporting documents within the framework of the CC standards. The Smart Card Industry has proven that the CC can provide value to consumers and vendors alike.

Perhaps if vendors, evaluation labs, government and customers came together in international communities, more of us can all realize greater value in CC evaluations. However, in order to realize this greater value, vendors would have to invest more time and effort in participating in these international forums and standards bodies. In order for vendors to justify this increased investment, there must be a visible return-on-investment in the form of increased revenue or reduced development and support costs. The leaders will need to develop a way to justify these investments to improve the Common Criteria so that more customers and vendors will benefit.

The current (as of June 2010) working groups established by the Common Criteria Development Board (CCDB) and the protection profile (PP) development working groups established by NIAP have encouraged greater vendor participation than in the past. Vendors should take advantage of these opportunities to ensure that vendors and customer interests are being met. I believe that by working collaboratively, CC can evolve into a much more valuable tool towards meeting our customers' security assurance requirements.

Glossary of Terms and Abbreviations

Accreditation
Common Criteria (CC) testing and evaluation laboratories (CCTL) are accredited by national government agencies to conduct CC evaluations. Accreditation involves meeting quality process standards and demonstrated expertise in CC evaluations. FIPS 140 labs are also accredited using similar standards.

Architecture
Target of Evaluation (TOE) architecture refers to the high-level structure and design of the product including its major modules and interfaces. The Architecture may also include specific technologies used in the TOE.

Assurance
Assurance is confidence that the Target of Evaluation (TOE) or product will operate securely. Assurance is gained by independent, third-party evaluation against internationally-recognized security standards.

Assurance Maintenance
Maintaining the security assurance achieved by Common Criteria (CC) evaluations is important to customers deploying and using the evaluated products. Assurance Maintenance is a mechanism used to provide on-going assurance after an initial CC evaluation.

Augmentation
Security Assurance Requirements (SAR) contained in standard Evaluation Assurance Levels (EAL) may be augmented with additional SARs. For example, many products have been evaluated at EAL 4 augmented with ALC_FLR.2, Flaw Remediation. This adds the ALC_FLR.2 requirement to the standard set of SARs in EAL 4 to the evaluation.

Best Practices
Practices become known as Best Practices when they have proven to be particularly effective. Best Practices have been demonstrated to be effective in a number of circumstances and environments.

Block Diagram
A product or Target of Evaluation (TOE) architecture can be depicted in a block diagram. The block diagram decomposes the TOE into its major modules and their interfaces.

Buy Versus Build
Buy versus Build decisions are made to determine whether it is better to purchase outsourced services or products over using in-house resources to perform the service or deliver the product. The Buy-versus-Build analysis requires consideration of several factors including costs and benefits.

Certificate-Authorizing
Fourteen nations that participate in the Common Criteria Mutual Recognition Agreement (CCRA) have qualified to issue or authorize Common Criteria certificates. These nations accredit evaluation laboratories and evaluation validation resources.

Certificate-Consuming
All nations that participate in the Common Criteria Mutual Recognition Agreement (CCRA) are Certificate-Consuming and recognize certificates that are issued by any of the certificate-authorizing nations.

Certification
Certification (or validation) marks the final, official completion of a successful Common Criteria evaluation. The national certificate-authorizing body certifies the results of the evaluation laboratory and issues a certificate to the sponsor (vendor).

Class, Family, Component, Element
Security Functional Requirements and Security Assurance Requirements are organized hierarchically into classes, families, components, and elements with each level defining greater specificity and details of each requirement.

Common Criteria Development Board (CCDB)
Composed of Common Criteria national Scheme representatives, the Common Criteria Development Board (CCDB) is responsible for the ongoing evolution and management of the Common Criteria standards.

The CCDB review potential changes to the standard and sponsor working groups to develop solutions.

Common Criteria Evaluation and Validation Scheme (CCEVS)
The U.S. National Information Assurance Partnership (NIAP) operates the U.S. Common Criteria national Scheme known as Common Criteria Evaluation and Validation Scheme (CCEVS). CCEVS manages the validation effort for all evaluations conducted in the U.S.

Common Criteria (Mutual) Recognition Agreement (CCRA)
Each member country participating in the Common Criteria has signed the Common Criteria (Mutual) Recognition Agreement (CCRA) which defines the rules of the use and recognition of any certificate issued by a certificate-authorizing nation by all certificate-consuming nations.

Common Criteria Vendors' Forum (CCVF)
The Common Criteria Vendors' Forum is an ad hoc organization of commercial product vendor company representatives gathered to discuss Common Criteria and CC-related issues, develop solutions and drive action to improve CC. They accomplish this by creating awareness of the issues and to provide a single voice as a vendor community to the standards bodies and policy makers

Common Evaluation Methodology
The Common Evaluation Methodology (CEM) defines the requirements of the evaluator for CC evaluations. This standard along with supporting documents (SD) and protection profiles (PP) help ensure consistent evaluations around the world.

Configuration
Configuration refers to the settings or customization of products for use in customer environments. These configuration settings adjust for the unique deployment environment. Inappropriate security settings may result in exploitable vulnerabilities.

Configuration Management
Product configuration management (CM) controls and organizes the components of the product to ensure that all of the correct component versions are used to build the product. For software products, configu-

ration management is usually managed by source code control tools such as CVS or Perforce.

Due Diligence

Due diligence is the practice of carefully examining alternatives before committing to purchase. Vendors will practice due diligence prior to selecting evaluation labs or consultants. This examination will include assessments across a variety of categories including: price, technical expertise, demonstrated experience and quality.

Evaluation

Evaluation is the examination of evidence by independent, accredited third-party testing laboratories. Independent examination against international standards is the foundation for the Common Criteria (CC). Security assurance is derived through evaluation.

Evaluation Assurance Level

The Evaluation Assurance Level (EAL) defines the depth of the evaluator examination. EALs are comprised of a set of Security Assurance Requirements (SAR). There are 7 EALs with EAL 1 being the least stringent and EAL 7 being the most stringent.

Evaluation Test Report

The Evaluation Test Reports (ETR) are written by the evaluation lab recording their findings during their evaluation. Evaluation labs will generate interim ETRs as well as a final ETR that are reviewed by the validators or certifiers.

Explicitly-Stated Requirements

Customized Security Functional Requirements (SFR) or Security Assurance Requirements (SAR) may be developed if the standard SFRs or SARs as defined in Common Criteria Parts 2 and 3 (respectively) do not apply to the Target of Evaluation (TOE).

Federal Information Processing Standard 140

Federal Information Processing Standard 140 (FIPS 140) is the standard maintained by the U.S. National Institute of Standards and Technology (NIST) and the Canadian Communications Security Establishment (CSE) pertaining to cryptographic module standards.

Flaw Remediation

Flaw Remediation is more commonly known as bug fixing. Flaw remediation refers to the entire process of reporting defects, developing patches or fixes, deploying the patches to affected systems, and advising customers.

Functional Specification

Functional Specification (FSP) documents describe the functions of the product or Target of Evaluation (TOE). The FSP provides a high-level description of what capabilities the product provides.

Impact Analysis Report

An Impact Analysis Report (IAR) describes the changes made to a previously-evaluated Target of Evaluation (TOE) along with an analysis of how these changes have an impact on the security evaluation result. If the changes can be shown to not impact the security claims of the evaluation, assurance can be maintained.

Implementation Representation

In software terms, Implementation Representation is the source code.

In Evaluation

There is no internationally recognized definition for In Evaluation but generally speaking when a Security Target has been approved for evaluation, the validation Scheme will recognize the Target of Evaluation (TOE) as being In Evaluation status.

Information Technology

Information Technology (IT) is the general term used for computers, electronic data storage, networking, operating systems, databases, application software and other technologies used to process, transmit, and store electronic information.

Intellectual Property

Intellectual Property (IP) is the knowledge or technology owned by an organization. IP generally has some competitive value and must be protected in order to maintain a competitive advantage in the market-place.

International Common Criteria Conference

The International Common Criteria Conference (ICCC) is the annual conference hosted by one of the Common Criteria Mutual Recognition Agreement (CCRA) member nations. The purpose of the ICCC is to share information about Common Criteria-related activities including: new developments, applications of CC, and new opportunities.

Interpretations

The Common Criteria (CC) standards were designed to be quite flexible and as such are subject to interpretation by national Schemes in order to meet local requirements and regulations. Each national Scheme is responsible for managing interpretations for use by evaluators and validators.

Intrusion Detection System

An Intrusion Detection System (IDS) is a security device or technology that detects access to protected information or systems. Network IDS monitor networks for activity that may be malicious. Host-based IDS monitor computer systems for potentially malicious activity.

Kickoff Meeting

The Kickoff Meeting is the initial formal meeting between the validators, evaluators and sponsor (vendor). The Kickoff Meeting is intended to formally start the evaluation and validation effort. This marks the commitment of the necessary resources from all parties. It also sets the parameters for the evaluation effort in terms of scope and timeframe.

Letter of Intent

A Letter of Intent (LOI) is a letter usually written on company letterhead signed by an official of the company indicating that company's commitment to proceeding with a Common Criteria (CC) evaluation. The LOI usually includes details on the product, product version, planned Evaluation Assurance Level (EAL), and any applicable Protection Profile (PP) conformance claims.

Observation Report

Evaluators generate Observation Reports (OR) to record issues or comments they observe during the evaluation of evidence. ORs may note discrepancies or incomplete information in evidence documents.

Vendors are expected to respond to ORs in order for the evaluation to continue.

Outsource
Outsourcing refers to the act of employing resources outside of one's own organization to perform a service or deliver an output. Contrasted with in-house development, outsourcing employs a third-party.

Platforms
Platforms refer to the computing base upon which application software will execute. The Platform may be viewed as the dependencies of the application software including: operating system, computer hardware and networking.

Protection Profile
Protection Profiles (PP) are documents intended to reflect customer security requirements for a particular technology type. PPs contain security functional requirements (SFR) and security assurance requirements (SAR) or Evaluation Assurance Level (EAL). Targets of Evaluation (TOE) may evaluate against the requirements within a PP and claim compliance to the PP by meeting all of the evaluation requirements in the PP.

Quality Assurance
Quality Assurance (QA) is a function within the developer organization chartered with the responsibility for establishing and executing product quality practices. The QA team is usually responsible for developing and executing product tests.

Rework
Rework refers to the editing and re-examination of Common Criteria (CC) evaluation evidence due to errors or omissions in the original evidence. Evidence documents are submitted to evaluators for their review and judgment. Should the evidence fail to meet the requirements of the evaluation, evaluators will return the evidence to the authors with comments in the form of Observation Reports (OR). The evidence authors are expected to rework the evidence and re-submit the revision for re-evaluation.

Scheme
Each member nation of the Common Criteria Mutual Recognition Agreement (CCRA) has a governing body or Scheme. The Scheme is responsible for representing that nation's interests in the Common Criteria (CC). The Scheme manages the validators.

Secure Development
Secure Development is the set of practices believed to result in a more secure product. These practices may include: security training, use of security tools, security testing and use of secure coding practices.

Security Assurance Requirement
Security Assurance Requirements (SAR) are defined in Common Criteria standard part 3. SARs define the product development, delivery and installation processes. SARs are conveniently organized into sets called Evaluation Assurance Levels (EAL).

Security Functional Requirement
Security Functional Requirements (SFR) are defined in Common Criteria standard part 2. SFRs define the product's security features. SFRs may be Explicitly-Stated or customized if the standard SFRs do not fit the Target of Evaluation.

Security Target
The Security Target (ST) is the foundational document of the Common Criteria (CC) evaluation. The ST defines what will be evaluated and to what depth. The ST contains all of the security claims for the Target of Evaluation (TOE). All subsequent evidence must be consistent with the ST claims.

Site Visit
Evaluators are required to conduct first-hand examinations of certain tools and procedures used by vendors during their development processes. Evaluators conduct these first-hand examinations during vendor development site visits.

Supporting Document
Supporting Documents (SD) are auxiliary documents developed to provide greater guidance for evaluators. The Smart Card Industry has

developed several SDs to provide more detailed instruction for evaluators on how to test smart card devices.

Switching Costs
Switching Costs are the costs incurred due to switching from one provider to another. These costs may include the time required for the new provider to be sufficiently knowledgeable about the technologies and processes used to be as effective as the previous provider.

Time and Materials
Time and Materials (T&M) contracts are set up whereby the provider is paid based on the time and materials actually spend on a project. The customer only pays for what has been used. Fixed price contracts are an alternative.

Time-to-Market
Time-to-Market (TTM) is the concept that products that are introduced into the marketplace ahead of the competition enjoy a revenue generation advantage. TTM drives product vendors to try to be first on the market with a new product or new capability.

TOE Boundary
The Target of Evaluation (TOE) Boundary sets the physical and logical limits of the evaluation. The TOE Boundary is defined in the Security Target (ST) document to advise evaluators and consumers what is included in the evaluation.

TOE Security Functionality
The Target of Evaluation Security Functionality (TSF) is the total security capability claimed by the Target of Evaluation (TOE). The TSF must meet the requirements of all of the claimed Security Functional Requirements (SFR) in the Security Target (ST) document.

Validation
Validation (or certification) is the final, official completion of a successful Common Criteria evaluation. The national certificate-authorizing body certifies the results of the evaluation laboratory and issues a certificate to the sponsor (vendor). The United States tends to use the term validation over certification.

Version

A Version is a uniquely identifiable variation or revision of a product. Common Criteria evaluations are valid only for a specified version of a product. That version is specified in the Security Target document.

Vulnerabilities

Vulnerabilities are security flaws or weaknesses that may be accidentally or maliciously exploited to expose unauthorized access to data or systems.

Abbreviations

CAP	Composed Assurance Package	NIST	National Institute of Standards and Technology
CAPP	Controlled-Access Protection Profile	OR	Observation Report
CC	Common Criteria	OS	Operating System
CCDB	Common Criteria Development Board	OSP	Organizational Security Policy
CCEVS	Common Criteria Evaluation and Validation Scheme	PKI	Public Key Infrastructure
CCRA	Common Criteria (Mutual) Recognition Agreement	PM	Product Manager
CCVF	Common Criteria Vendors' Forum	POC	Point of Contact
CEM	Common Evaluation Methodology	PP	Protection Profile
CM	Configuration Management	QA	Qualtiy Assurance
CMVP	Cryptographic Module Validation Program	ROI	Return on Investment
CSE	Communications Securtiy Establishment	SAR	Security Assurance Requirement
EAL	Evaluation Assurance Level	SD	Supporting Document
ETR	Evaluation Test Report	SEP	Symantec Endpoint Protection
EWP	Evaluation Work Plan	SFR	Security Functional Requirement
FIPS	Federal Information Processing Standard	SPD	Security Problem Definition
FSP	Functional Specificaiton	ST	Security Target
IAR	Impact Analysis Report	T&M	Time and Materials
ICCC	International Common Criteria Conference	TOE	Target of Evaluation
IDS	Intrusion Detection System	TSF	TOE Security Functionality
IP	Intellectual Property	TSFI	TSF Interface
IT	Information Technology	TSS	TOE Summary Specification
MRE	Medium Robustness Environment	TTM	Time-to-Market
NIAP	National Information Assurance Partnership	US-CERT	United States Computer Emergency Readiness Team

References

[Applus 2008] Applus. "Automated tools for supporting CC design evidence." September 2008.
<http://www.commoncriteriaportal.org/iccc/9iccc/pdf/A2503.pdf>

[Arnold 2006] Arnold, James. "Impacts of Third-Party Consultants on Common Criteria Assurances." September 2006.
<http://www.commoncriteriaportal.org/iccc/7iccc/t3/t3191530.pdf>

[atsec] atsec. "Common Criteria: National Validation Scheme Differences: CCEVS, CSEC and BSI." 29 April 2009.
<http://www.atsec.com/downloads/documents/Scheme_diffs_09-04-29-2.pdf>

[Australiasia] Australasia Scheme
<http://www.dsd.gov.au/infosec/evaluation_services/aisep_pages/aisep.html>

[Bidstrup] Bidstrup, Eric . "Common Criteria and answering the question 'Is it Safe' ." Thursday, December 20, 2007.
<http://blogs.msdn.com/sdl/archive/2007/12/20/common-criteria-and-answering-the-question-is-it-safe.aspx>

[BSI] BSI website (English)
<https://www.bsi.bund.de/cln_156/EN/TheBSI/thebsi_node.html>

[CC Portal] Common Criteria Portal
<http://www.commoncriteriaportal.org>

[CC Standards] Common Criteria Standards Parts 1,2, 3 and CEM
<http://www.commoncriteriaportal.org/thecc.html>

[CCVF] Common Criteria Vendors' Forum
<http://www.ccvendorforum.org>

[CMVP] Cryptographic Module Validation Program
<http://csrc.nist.gov/groups/STM/cmvp/index.html>

[Connor 2007] Connor, Erin. "Developer Documentation – A Who To Guide." September 2007. <http://www.8iccc.com/media/doc/Developer%20Documentation%20-%20A%20Who%20To%20Guide_ErinConnor.pdf>

[Dale] Dale, Audrey. IAPB Briefing. 23 March 2006. <http://csrc.nist.gov/groups/SMA/ispab/documents/minutes/2006-03/A_Dale-March2006-ISPAB.pdf>

[Davidson] Jackson, William. "Mary Ann Davidson: In defense of common criteria." *Government Computer News*. 7 October 2007. <http://gcn.com/Articles/2007/10/07/Mary-Ann-Davidson--In-defense-of-common-criteria.aspx?Page=1>

[Developer] BSI. "Guidelines for Developer Documentation." 2007. <https://www.bsi-fuer-buerger.de/cae/servlet/contentblob/479428/publicationFile/30258/CommonCriteriaDevelopersGuide_pdf.pdf>

[Eurosmart] Eurosmart <http://www.eurosmart.com/>

[Forge 2009] Forge, Françoise. "Monitoring Common Criteria for Smart Card Devices." September 2009. <http://www.yourcreativesolutions.nl/ICCC10/proceedings/doc/pp/ISCI_monitoring%20CC_For_SmartSecurityDevices.pdf>

[France] French CC Evidence Example <http://www.ssi.gouv.fr/archive/fr/documentation/exemple/index-en.html>

[Guthrie] Guthrie, Priscilla. National Information Assurance Acquisition Policy. 6 August 2002

[ISO] ISO/IEC Directives, Part 2 <http://www.iso.org>

[Kickoff] NIAP Kickoff Meeting Agenda < http://www.niap-ccevs.org/forms/T6006.pdf >

[Krause 2007] Krause, Christian. "Guideline for Developer Documentation." September 2007.
<http://www.8iccc.com/media/doc/Guideline%20for%20Developer%20Documentation_Krause%20Christian.ppt>

[Medefesser 2007] Medefesser, Jane. "Vendor Strategies for maximizing process under the Common Criteria." Septermber 2007.
<http://www.8iccc.com/media/doc/Vendor%20strategies%20for%20maximizing%20process%20under%20the%20Common%20Criteria_Medefesser%20Jane.pdf>

[NCSP] National Cyber Security Partnership
<http://www.cyberpartnership.org/init-tech.html>

[NIAP] National Information Assurance Partnership
<http://www.niap-ccevs.org/>

[NSTISSP] NSTISSP #11
<http://www.niap-ccevs.org/nstissp_11_revised_factsheet.pdf>

[Oracle] Oracle Software Security Assurance Process
<http://www.oracle.com/security/docs/software-security-assurance.pdf>

[OWASP] OWASP Top 10
<http://www.owasp.org/index.php/Category:OWASP_Top_Ten_Project>

[Pattinson 2007] Pattinson, Fiona. "Common Criteria in the Real World." September 2007.
<http://www.8iccc.com/media/doc/Common%20Criteria%20in%20the%20Real%20World_Pattinson%20Fiona.ppt>

[SDLC] Microsoft SDLC
<http://blogs.msdn.com/sdl/default.aspx>

[Stodart 2008] Stodart, Tyrone. "Common Criteria Works! (How the Smart Card Industry Uses the CC)." September 2008.
<http://www.commoncriteriaportal.org/iccc/9iccc/pdf/B2501.pdf>

[stratsec 2008] stratsec. "Realising benefit and value from CC evaluations." September 2008. <http://www.commoncriteriaportal.org/iccc/9iccc/pdf/C2302.pdf>

[Symantec] Jackson, Joab. "Symantec: Common Criteria is bad for you." *Government Computer News.* 4 May 2007. <http://gcn.com/Articles/2007/05/04/Symantec>

[Tanaka 2008] Tanaka, Masashi. "A smart card evaluation experience under a Japanese scheme." September 2008. <http://www.commoncriteriaportal.org/iccc/9iccc/pdf/B2502.pdf>

[UK] CESG UK Scheme <http://www.cesg.gov.uk/products_services/iacs/cc_and_itsec/index.shtml>

[Under Attack] Jackson, William. "Under attack: Common Criteria has loads of critics, but is it getting a bum rap?" *Government Computer News.* 13 August 2007 <http://gcn.com/Articles/2007/08/10/Under-attack.aspx?Page=1>

Recent Evaluations

The following products have completed CC evaluations under the CC version 3.1 standards. This information was harvested from the Common Criteria Portal website in April 2010. Each entry includes the product name, manufacturer, certification date, and any Protection Profile compliance claims. I've added the validating Scheme and evaluation lab so that you can see which entities are the most active. I've also listed the Security Target author so you can see who are using third-party or evaluation lab services to produce these documents and which vendors are writing their own STs.

Access Control

Name	SafeGuard Enterprise Device Encryption, Version 5.30
Manufacturer	Utimaco Safeware AG
EAL	EAL 3+
PP	None
Cert. Date	2-Oct-09
Scheme	Germany
Evaluation Lab	SRC
ST Author	Utimaco

Name	RSA Access Manager v6.1
Manufacturer	RSA, The Security Division of EMC
EAL	EAL 3+
PP	US Authorization Server PP
Cert. Date	16-Nov-09
Scheme	Canada
Evaluation Lab	EWA-Canada
ST Author	Corsec

Name	CA Access Control r12 sp1
Manufacturer	CA, Inc.
EAL	EAL 3+
PP	None
Cert. Date	16-Dec-09

Scheme	US
Evaluation Lab	Booz Allen Hamilton
ST Author	Booz Allen Hamilton

Boundary Protection

Name	Fort Fox Hardware Data Diode, versie FFHDD2
Manufacturer	Fox-IT B.V.
EAL	EAL 4+
PP	None
Cert. Date	7-Sep-09
Scheme	The Netherlands
Evaluation Lab	Brightsight BV
ST Author	Fox-IT

Name	GeNUScreen 2.0
Manufacturer	GeNUA für Gesellschaft Netzwerk- und UNIX-Administration mbH
EAL	EAL 4+
PP	None
Cert. Date	12-Oct-09
Scheme	Germany
Evaluation Lab	Tele-Consulting
ST Author	GeNUA

Name	RSA enVision platform v4.0 SP 1
Manufacturer	RSA, The Security Division of EMC
EAL	EAL 3+
PP	None
Cert. Date	22-Jan-10
Scheme	Canada
Evaluation Lab	EWA-Canada
ST Author	Corsec

Databases

Category	DB
Name	Oracle Database 11g Enterprise Edition, Release 11.1.0.7 with Critical Patch Updates up to and including July 2009

Manufacturer	Oracle Corporation
EAL	EAL 4+
PP	None
Cert. Date	16-Sep-09
Scheme	Germany
Evaluation Lab	atsec
ST Author	atsec, Oracle

Name	Oracle Database 11g Enterprise Edition with Oracle Label Security, Release 11.1.0.7 with Critical Patch Updates up to and including July 2009
Manufacturer	Oracle Corporation
EAL	EAL 4+
PP	None
Cert. Date	16-Sep-09
Scheme	Germany
Evaluation Lab	atsec
ST Author	atsec, Oracle

Detection Devices

Name	NitroSecurity Intrusion Prevention System v8.0.0
Manufacturer	NitroSecurity, Inc.
EAL	EAL 3+
PP	US IDS System PP
Cert. Date	27-Oct-09
Scheme	US
Evaluation Lab	SAIC
ST Author	SAIC

Name	Tenable Security Center 3.2 (SC3) with 3D Tool 1.2 (3DT), Log Correlation Engine 2.0.2 (LCE), Passive Vulnerability Scanner 3.0 (PVS), and Nessus Scanner 3.0.4 (Nessus)
Manufacturer	Tenable Network Security, Inc.
EAL	EAL 2+
PP	US IDS System PP
Cert. Date	31-Jan-10
Scheme	US
Evaluation Lab	SAIC
ST Author	SAIC

Data Guards

Name	Luna PCI Configured for Use in Luna SA 4.1 with Backup
Manufacturer	SafeNet Inc.
EAL	EAL 4+
PP	Cryptographic Module for CSP Signing Operations with Backup PP
Cert. Date	12-Nov-09
Scheme	The Netherlands
Evaluation Lab	Brightsight BV
ST Author	SafeNet

Data Protection

Name	IBM WebSphere Portal 6.0
Manufacturer	IBM corporation
EAL	EAL 4
PP	None
Cert. Date	25-Sep-09
Scheme	US
Evaluation Lab	SAIC
ST Author	SAIC

Name	Cruzer Enterprise FIPS Edition, firmware v6.612 and v6.615
Manufacturer	SanDisk
EAL	EAL 2+
PP	None
Cert. Date	28-Sep-09
Scheme	Australasia
Evaluation Lab	stratsec
ST Author	SanDisk

Name	Cisco IronPort S-Series Web Security Appliance (WSA) (S160, S360, S660) running AsyncOS 5.6.1
Manufacturer	Cisco Systems, Inc.
EAL	EAL 2
PP	None
Cert. Date	20-Oct-09
Scheme	US

Evaluation Lab	SAIC
ST Author	SAIC

Name	Trusted Client v2.3
Manufacturer	Becrypt Limited
EAL	EAL 2
PP	None
Cert. Date	5-Nov-09
Scheme	Australasia
Evaluation Lab	stratsec
ST Author	Becrypt

Smart Cards and IC's

Name	Sony Smartcard RC-S251/SO2 version 1.0
Manufacturer	Sony Corporation
EAL	EAL 4+
PP	None
Cert. Date	3-Sep-09
Scheme	Spain
Evaluation Lab	LGAI-APPLUS
ST Author	Sony

Name	ID-One Cosmo V7.0-a SmartCard in configuration Large Dual, Large and Standard Dual
Manufacturer	Oberthur Technologies / ATMEL Secure Microcontroller Solutions
EAL	EAL 5+
PP	Java Card System PP
Cert. Date	29-Sep-09
Scheme	France
Evaluation Lab	Thales-Ceaci
ST Author	Oberthur

Name	MTCOS Pro 2.1 EAC / P5CD080/CZ
Manufacturer	MaskTech International GmbH
EAL	EAL 4+
PP	Machine Readable Travel Document with ICAO Application Extended Access Control
Cert. Date	30-Sep-09

Scheme	Germany
Evaluation Lab	SRC
ST Author	MaskTech

Name	Electronic Health Card and SSCD Version 2.10
Manufacturer	Gemalto
EAL	EAL 4+
PP	Electronic Health Card PP
Cert. Date	7-Oct-09
Scheme	Germany
Evaluation Lab	TUV
ST Author	Gemalto

Name	TCOS Passport Version 2.0 Release 2/P5CD080V0B Extended Access Control Version 2.0.2.m3
Manufacturer	T-Systems Enterprise Services GmbH
EAL	EAL 4+
PP	Machine Readable Travel Document with ICAO Application Extended Access Control
Cert. Date	14-Oct-09
Scheme	Germany
Evaluation Lab	TUV
ST Author	T-Systems

Name	FS Sigma Version 01.01.05
Manufacturer	Toshiba Corporation
EAL	EAL 4+
PP	SmartCard IC Platform PP
Cert. Date	27-Oct-09
Scheme	the Netherlands
Evaluation Lab	Brightsight BV
ST Author	Toshiba

Name	JCLX80jTOP20ID : Java Trusted Open Platform IFX#v42, with patch version 2.0, embedded on SLE66CLX800PE or SLE66CLX360PE
Manufacturer	Trusted Logic / Infineon
EAL	EAL 5+
PP	None
Cert. Date	27-Oct-09

Scheme	France
Evaluation Lab	Serma Technologies
ST Author	Trusted Logic
Name	NXP MIFARE Plus MF1PLUSx0y1
Manufacturer	NXP Semiconductors Germany GmbH
EAL	EAL 4+
PP	Security IC Platform PP
Cert. Date	2-Nov-09
Scheme	Germany
Evaluation Lab	T-Systems
ST Author	NXP
Name	S3CC9PF 16-bit RISC Microcontroller for Smart Card, Revision 2
Manufacturer	Samsung Electronics Co., Ltd.
EAL	EAL 5+
PP	Security IC Platform PP
Cert. Date	4-Nov-09
Scheme	Germany
Evaluation Lab	TUV
ST Author	Samsung
Name	NXP Smart Card Controller P5CD081V1A and its major configurations P5CC081V1A, P5CN081V1A, P5CD041V1A, P5CD021V1A and P5CD016V1A each with IC dedicated Software
Manufacturer	NXP Semiconductors Germany GmbH
EAL	EAL 5+
PP	Security IC Platform PP
Cert. Date	10-Nov-09
Scheme	Germany
Evaluation Lab	T-Systems
ST Author	NXP
Name	ID-One Cosmo V7.0-n SmartCard in configuration Basic on NXP P5CC037 V0A
Manufacturer	Oberthur Card System / Philips (NXP)
EAL	EAL 5+
PP	Java Card System PP

Cert. Date	19-Nov-09
Scheme	France
Evaluation Lab	Thales-Ceaci
ST Author	Oberthur
Name	S3CC91A 16-bit RISC Microcontroller for Smart Card, Revision 7 with optional Secure RSA Crypto Library and specific IC Dedicated Software
Manufacturer	Samsung Electronics Co., Ltd.
EAL	EAL 5+
PP	SmartCard IC Platform PP
Cert. Date	20-Nov-09
Scheme	Germany
Evaluation Lab	TUV
ST Author	Samsung
Name	MICARDO V3.5 R1.0 eHC V1.0
Manufacturer	Sagem Orga GmbH
EAL	EAL 4+
PP	Electronic Health Card PP
Cert. Date	27-Nov-09
Scheme	Germany
Evaluation Lab	SRC
ST Author	Sagem Orga
Name	Infineon Smart Card IC (Security Controller) SLE66CX680PE / M1534-a14, SLE66CX360PE / M1536-a14, SLE66CX182PE / M1564-a14, SLE66CX480PE / M1565-a14 and SLE66CX482PE / M1577-a14 all with optional libraries RSA V1.6, EC V1.1, SHA-2 V1.0 and with specific IC dedicated software
Manufacturer	Infineon Technologies AG
EAL	EAL 5+
PP	SmartCard IC Platform PP
Cert. Date	3-Dec-09
Scheme	Germany
Evaluation Lab	TUV
ST Author	Infineon
Name	Sm@rtCafe Expert Version 5.0

Manufacturer	Giesecke & Devrient GmbH
EAL	EAL 4+
PP	Java Card System PP
Cert. Date	17-Dec-09
Scheme	Germany
Evaluation Lab	TUV
ST Author	Giesecke & Devrien

Name	CC IDeal Pass Passport (on SB23YR80A), version 1.3.3
Manufacturer	Sagem securite / STMicroelectronics
EAL	EAL 4+
PP	Machine Readable Travel Document with ICAO Application Basic Access Control
Cert. Date	21-Dec-09
Scheme	France
Evaluation Lab	CEI-LEYI
ST Author	Sagem Orga

Network Security

Name	CA Spectrum Network Fault Manager r9.0 SP1
Manufacturer	CA Incorporated
EAL	EAL 2
PP	None
Cert. Date	8-Sep-09
Scheme	Canada
Evaluation Lab	EWA-Canada
ST Author	Booz Allen Hamilton

Name	Microsoft System Center Mobile Device Manager 2008
Manufacturer	Microsoft Corporation
EAL	EAL 4+
PP	None
Cert. Date	17-Sep-09
Scheme	Australasia
Evaluation Lab	stratsec
ST Author	stratsec

Name	EMC VoyenceControl v4.1.0
Manufacturer	EMC Corporation
EAL	EAL 2+
PP	None
Cert. Date	25-Sep-09
Scheme	Canada
Evaluation Lab	EWA-Canada
ST Author	Corsec

Name	CypherNET Ethernet Encryptor (2.0.0), CypherNET Fibre Channel Encryptor (2.0.0), CypherStream Ethernet Encryptor (1.0.6) and CypherManager (6.5.0)
Manufacturer	Senetas Corporation Ltd.
EAL	EAL 4+
PP	None
Cert. Date	26-Oct-09
Scheme	Australasia
Evaluation Lab	CSC
ST Author	Senetas

Name	BladeLogic Operations Manager 7.4
Manufacturer	BladeLogic, Inc.
EAL	EAL 3
PP	None
Cert. Date	11-Nov-09
Scheme	US
Evaluation Lab	Booz Allen Hamilton
ST Author	Booz Allen Hamilton

Name	Trustwave Network Access Control (NAC) Software Version 3.4.0
Manufacturer	Trustwave
EAL	EAL 2+
PP	None
Cert. Date	12-Nov-09
Scheme	Canada
Evaluation Lab	DOMUS

Other Devices

Name	Fuji Xerox ApeosPort-IV C5570/C4470/C3370/C2270 DocuCentre-IV C5570/C4470/C3370/C2270 Series Controller Software Version:Controller ROM Ver.1.0.6
Manufacturer	Fuji Xerox Co., Ltd.
EAL	EAL 3
PP	None
Cert. Date	15-Oct-09
Scheme	Japan
Evaluation Lab	IT Security Center
ST Author	Fuji Xerox

Name	Oce PRISMAsync 11.9.75.55 as used in the Oce VarioPrint 41x0 Release 1.3
Manufacturer	OCE Technologies B.V.
EAL	EAL 2+
PP	None
Cert. Date	13-Nov-09
Scheme	Germany
Evaluation Lab	Brightsight BV
ST Author	Brightsight BV

Name	Microsoft Exchange Server 2007 Enterprise Edition (English), Version/Build 08.02.0176.002
Manufacturer	Microsoft Corporation
EAL	EAL 4+
PP	None
Cert. Date	16-Nov-09
Scheme	Germany
Evaluation Lab	TUV
ST Author	Microsoft

Name	bizhub C360 / bizhub C280 / bizhub C220 / ineo+ 360 / ineo+ 280 / ineo+ 220 / VarioLink 3622c / VarioLink 2822c / VarioLink 2222c Control Software Version:A0ED0Y0-0100-GM0-12
Manufacturer	Konica Minolta Business Technologies, Inc

EAL	EAL 3
PP	None
Cert. Date	30-Nov-09
Scheme	Japan
Evaluation Lab	Mizuho
ST Author	Konica

Name	1E Power and Patch Management Pack including WakeUp and NightWatchman Version 5.6 running on multiple platforms
Manufacturer	1E Ltd
EAL	EAL 2
PP	None
Cert. Date	18-Dec-09
Scheme	UK
Evaluation Lab	SiVenture
ST Author	SiVenture

Operating Systems

Name	Microsoft Windows Mobile 6.1
Manufacturer	Microsoft Corporation
EAL	EAL 4+
PP	None
Cert. Date	17-Sep-09
Scheme	Australasia
Evaluation Lab	stratsec
ST Author	stratsec

Name	NetApp Data ONTAP Version 7.3.1.1
Manufacturer	NetApp, Inc.
EAL	EAL 3+
PP	None
Cert. Date	5-Nov-09
Scheme	Canada
Evaluation Lab	DOMUS
ST Author	NetApp

Name	Hewlett-Packard HP-UX 11i v3 (using CCv3.1)

Manufacturer	Hewlett Packard Company
EAL	EAL 4+
PP	None
Cert. Date	27-Nov-09
Scheme	UK
Evaluation Lab	Logica
ST Author	HP

Name	Red Hat Enterprise Linux Ver. 5.3 on Dell 11G Family Servers
Manufacturer	Dell, Inc.
EAL	EAL 4+
PP	US Controlled Access PP
Cert. Date	23-Dec-09
Scheme	US
Evaluation Lab	atsec
ST Author	atsec, Dell

Name	Apple Mac OS X 10.6
Manufacturer	Apple Inc
EAL	EAL 3+
PP	US Controlled Access PP
Cert. Date	8-Jan-10
Scheme	Germany
Evaluation Lab	atsec
ST Author	atsec, Oracle

Name	Microsoft Windows Mobile 6.5
Manufacturer	Microsoft Corporation
EAL	EAL 4+
PP	None
Cert. Date	5-Feb-10
Scheme	Australasia
Evaluation Lab	stratsec
ST Author	stratsec

Name	VMware ESX Server 3.5 and VirtualCenter 2.5
Manufacturer	VMware, Inc.
EAL	EAL 4+

PP	None
Cert. Date	9-Feb-10
Scheme	Canada
Evaluation Lab	EWA-Canada
ST Author	Corsec

Trusted Computing

Name	SLB9635TT1.2 / m1566a13 HW a13 / FW 03.17.0008.00
Manufacturer	Infineon Technologies AG
EAL	EAL 4+
PP	Trusted Computing Group Protection Profile PC Client Specific Trusted Platform Module TPM Family 1.2, Level 2
Cert. Date	20-Nov-09
Scheme	Germany
Evaluation Lab	TUV
ST Author	Infineon

Index